THIS
IS HOW YOU
PITCH

HOW TO **KICK ASS** IN YOUR **FIRST YEARS** OF **PR**

Ed Zitron

This Is How You Pitch: How to Kick Ass in Your First Years of PR
Copyright © 2013 by Sunflower Press

For information about this title or to order other books and/or electronic media, contact the publisher:
Sunflower Press
200 Viridian Drive
Muskegan, MI 49440

ISBNs:
978-0-989608046 Paperback

Printed in the United States of America
Cover and Interior design by: 1106 Design

table of contents

acknowledgments

I dedicate this book to the following people :

▶ Nils Parker and Derek Kreindler, the two men who helped
  me turn the vestigial ideas of this book into the thing you're
  reading.

▶ Dylan Love, who read so many drafts he probably questions
  my ability to write a cohesive sentence.

▶ Eric Kuhn, who supported me throughout many crises,
  both personal and professional, and remained a steadfast
  friend.

▶ David Gorodyansky, an inspirational guy and good source
  of excellent advice in business.

▶ Rip Empson, a mental and professional support who I'd
  probably have gone insane without. Great advice, terrible
  jokes.

► Phil Broughton, my best friend and ally throughout the many moments in which PR nearly turned me into a monster.

► James Altucher, who directly advised me and indirectly inspired me through his blogs and books.

► Chris Heintz, a great friend, a great coworker, and someone who worked on the early ideas that inspired this book. He also helped me learn to pitch.

► Jeff Lovari, the first guy to teach me about pitching and the world of PR in an honest way.

► Robert Leshner, an amazing client, a great friend, and someone who has sent me so much business that he's indirectly paid for my rent several times.

► Robert Levitan, for being a mentor, a friend, and a constant reminder that family comes first.

► Vikram Savkar, a great friend, a great client, and the most well-spoken and interesting person I've had the fortune of working with.

► Isaac Webster, for taking exactly one vacation in the year I've known him. Oh, and all the clients he's put on at Bloomberg.

► Any and all clients past, present, and future who have worked with me.

foreword

There was an awful picture circulating around the net a couple of years ago. A big dead snapper fish held with its mouth open, to reveal a hideous grinning parasite clamped to and entirely replacing the creature's tongue. The Cymothoa exigua sucks the blood from the tongue until the organ dies, but remains locked to the stump, acting as a working prosthesis for the tongue. The Cymothoa, a tough little crustacean, is actually stronger and harder than the original tongue.

That's sort of what a PR is like.

Nobody likes PRs, right? Those weird, glittering eyes, and the teeth that would chew the blood out of your hands if you'd let them. Sharp-mouthed things that want to gnaw the life-force from you and then spit it up into the thirsty holes of some vampire celebrity. A swarm of parasites, stuck to the arts, and yet providing new skin and useful tendrils.

This is a book on how to be a PR. If you read it on those terms, I'm sure you will learn very useful things and not want to kill yourself at all. Ed Zitron's been from the bottom of the shit bucket to the rarefied air at the top of it where you can hire your own shit flies to circle your turdy domain, and he knows what he's talking about. This is a great book for you.

I don't want to be a PR. I may as well have been sent a book on fly-fishing or seducing plant life. It's like giving me a kettle made out of butter.

The weird thing is, I found it riveting. Not least because Ed Zitron is a very funny writer. I mean, I don't necessarily want to say that this is the story of one man saying, "fuck it, I'm going to be the best horrible tongue parasite in the world!" But... kind of, in parts. It's as much Ed's personal story as it is a handbook to the very real world of reputation management.

This *is* a real world. I don't think it was necessarily intended, but a layman will gain more from this book, in terms of understanding and perceiving the state and motion of the professional world, than from *The Four-Hour Workweek*. It's an absolutely fascinating perspective on the way things are done, and I recommend it unreservedly as both entertainment and food for thought.

Disclosure: I can't afford a PR and I'm writing this foreword for free. Read the book to find out why I'm an idiot.

Warren Ellis
Author of *Gun Machine, Transmetropolitan* and
Dead Pig Collector

introduce yourself to PR

My first real experiences in PR came, ironically enough, on the other side of the fence. I was a reporter for a few publications, most notably *PC Zone*, the first PC gaming magazine in England. As you can imagine, the video game journalism community is quite small. There were maybe twenty-five PR people, and my publication only had four people on staff. It was a very small world indeed. Needless to say, PR people and reporters were relatively chummy in that particular field.

It helped that the PR people representing the game companies rarely needed to do much pitching. There weren't many people to pitch to, after all. And besides, the competition between the few of us journalists who were there was strong enough and the consumer demand for their products (and our analysis/ratings) was great enough that they were the proverbial hot girl at the dance, not us. A man in a suit would turn up, who you knew, and you'd like that man in a suit because he'd take you out for drinks and was a good chap. Sometimes you'd review his game badly because the game was bad, he'd be annoyed at you for a while, but at the end of the day it was all

1

just part of the job, and you accepted it like any other occupational hazard. Everybody was friendly. Reporters were happy to hear from the PR people, believe it or not.

It was there that I was able to see the PR chain in its "purest" form—a company has a product, they hire a PR person to promote that product, the PR person gets a writer to write about it, and a few days or weeks or months later, customers read about it. It was that simple. Or was it? I soon found out that my experience in England skewed the way I looked at things as far as the PR-media relationship goes.

Some time after my stint at *PC Zone*, I took a job with a PR firm in New York City. Before the big move from London, I would dream of taking people out for drinks and being called by reporters for the hot scoop on Samsung, or Amazon, or whoever my PR firm supposedly represented. I thought I would be the person everyone wanted to associate with. When I found out I got the job, I went and got blackout drunk to celebrate my initiation into a world of fabulous parties and adoring reporters.

I was horribly mistaken. In America, reporters treat PR people like pests. It's not hard to understand why. There are an estimated 313 million people in the US. There are 3.2 million results under "Public Relations" on LinkedIn. Under "reporter," there are 370,000, while "journalist" nets 339,000. "Writer" broadens it to 1.2 million. That's practically three-to-one PR to media. For every writer looking for a story, there are three PR people trying to make sure it's their client's story that the writer finds.

Sometimes people ask me, "Why not just take out an advertisement? Why bother with PR?" The answer is because people don't relate to advertisements (they consume them). They want to relate to stories, written by people smarter than them, experts like reporters and pundits. So few of the 3.2 million people in PR understand this. That's where you come in. Be better than the rest of the pack who dream about adoration and open bars. Learn how to work with reporters, how to make things mutually beneficial. And most importantly, learn how to pitch.

As Seen On TV

In Britain, where I originally hail from, our main television network, the BBC, is very different from America's main networks. Rather than rely on advertising, their entire budget comes from taxpayer money. In a country with 62 million people and fairly high taxes, that's a nice sum of money.

A lot of it goes to creating costume dramas and sitcoms with extremely dry humor, stuff that Americans consider to be unbearably boring. But one series has become extremely popular across the globe because it has a very universal premise. *Top Gear* is a show where three poorly dressed, out-of-shape, middle-aged men drive expensive cars around race tracks, take old beaters on transcontinental adventures, and lob insults at one another along the way.

The BBC has managed to license the show on every single continent and makes millions of dollars each year on license fees, merchandising, live events, and all sorts of other crap. It's so popular that even people who don't give a damn about cars (like me) know about it. The hosts, as a result, are A-list celebrities in the UK and abroad.

During the course of my work, I ran into somebody who, on the surface, seemed to be the "real-life" version of a *Top Gear* host. His job was to test drive cars and evaluate them for the manufacturers.

While trying to make small talk, I asked him if he was a fan of *Top Gear*. I may as well have asked him if he liked cat food sandwiches and banging his sister.

"Ed, you've seen *Sex and the City* before, right?"

"Of course not," I blatantly lied, breaking one of my cardinal rules of PR.

He wasn't falling for it. "Come on, we've all seen it, you and I both know that one of the characters, Samantha, that leathery cougar, is in PR."

"Uh huh."

"How many times has someone said to you, 'I really want to get into PR because I want to be like Samantha. I really want the lifestyle, the parties, the good-looking people, the free booze?'"

"Too many times to count," I replied. "And every time I tell them that it's just TV. It's a fake representation of PR."

His expression changed from one of bored detachment to engagement. "I'm glad you understand! It's exactly the same thing for me. Everybody thinks I'm out in Monaco driving a Ferrari around the harbor while a bunch of well-dressed Italians sit patiently waiting for my critique. Most of the time, I'm riding around in a Ford Focus, trying to figure out where that hissing wind noise is coming from at seventy-five miles per hour on the freeway. It's about as far from *Top Gear* as you can get. The 'made for TV moments' are maybe one to two percent of my job."

If you're one of those people who really wants to be the next Samantha, then stop. Put down this book. Get a job in a bar or a trendy new restaurant. You will meet lots of exciting, good-looking people and you will drink for free thanks to generous patrons and coworkers who will try to bed you.

I wish I could say that PR is as remotely exciting as working in a bar, or that it will be smooth sailing from here on out, but it never is. Unless you are born wealthy with a significant trust fund to draw on, the stressors of the job and the measly amount you're being paid to endure them combine to make the first few years a rough ride. On the other hand, if you are interested in helping people with complex problems, handling issues that require diplomacy, empathy, creativity, and even a bit of cunning, then keep reading. There's no better place to be. Especially if you have to work for a living.

And work you will. Every single job, whether you're a surgeon, a police officer, a test driver, or a PR person, has a lot of dry, unglamorous hard work involved. There is no escaping it. In PR especially, there is a lot of paper pushing, coffee drinking, and anxiety, while sleep, leisure time, and relaxation are limited to nonexistent, at least until you are established.

But that's what makes the "TV moments," like the parties, the cool and interesting people—and of course, the big payday—all the more satisfying. I'm not saying you have to do grunt work in order to "pay your dues" because "that's how it's always been." Don't misunderstand. What I'm telling you is that this is how you get good as a professional PR person.

So, What the Hell Is PR?

A lot of people will tell you, "I'm in PR". Most of them couldn't tell you what that even means. They'll start "umm"-ing and "uhh"-ing and spitting a bunch of jargon at you until, finally, you say, "That's cool," so they'll stop talking. Truthfully, there's nothing mysterious about Public Relations. It's all about how your client—whether it's a company, an individual, a foundation, a music group—relates to the public. Central to this is their reputation.

Reputation is the result—the consequence—of how your client relates to the public. Do they relate well? Then they are more likely to have a good reputation. Do they relate poorly? Well then, best of luck to you. This is not jargon or some set of esoteric buzzwords. You are literally the guardian of their reputation, an intangible that is so important no amount of money can purchase a good one or repair a bad one. To put it simply, if you are in PR, you are in the business of reputation management.

To get a sense for how important and universal this idea is to PR, take a second, close your eyes, and reach back into the deepest, darkest recesses of your mind. Think back to high school. For some of you, this will be a blissful time, in which case put the book down because I hate you. Just kidding...sort of. For most of us, high school is full of painful memories of awkwardness, rejection, alienation, and acne medication. Nowhere was that awkwardness and rejection more acutely apparent than in the cafeteria during lunch when you were trying to find a place to sit. It was an absolute minefield.

PR is a lot like navigating that cafeteria minefield in high school, except this time you're playing for keeps. And instead of trying to get a seat at the cool kids' lunch table for yourself, you're trying to help your client find a seat wherever their customers are—whether they're current loyalists or potential conquests. Sometimes, you will be representing the business-world equivalent of the mathletes or the theatre geeks; companies with middling or downright poor reputations that are looking to shed that image. In other cases, you'll be working with the literal new kids—companies that are just getting started and have no reputation at all.

Most of the time, you will be helping the shy, quiet kid get some well-deserved recognition. Maybe he has a middling reputation, or no reputation at all, but you and he both know all he needs is his time in the sun. Businesses need someone to show off their accomplishments or tell them how to discuss their accomplishments with more fire—or even which accomplishments are worth talking about. And sometimes, they need someone to cover for them when they make a mistake. Those are all key elements to reputation management and you are going to have to learn how to perform the duties related to each of them.

We live in an era of total media saturation: 24-hour cable news, high-speed internet, web-enabled smartphones, social media. And, if you'll allow me to flog our high school metaphor fully to death, the media *is* the cafeteria. All of its members are seated at their respective tables and they cannot wait to point and laugh when your poor client trips over his shoelaces and spills his milk all over himself. Sometimes it's so frustratingly predictable that you'll want to pick a fight with them to defend your client, to defend every client in the history of clients. You'll need to learn to resist that urge. Not just because the reputation you cultivate for yourself as a PR person transfers to your clients, but as you'll see later on in the book, because being nice to the media will actually pay dividends. They may not necessarily laugh at your client when they screw up. Or if they do, they'll laugh *with them,* not at them.

A good reputation means good standing for both your client *and* for you as a PR person. A good reputation not only helps your client make money, but when something does go wrong—and it will—a client with a good reputation, assisted by an excellent PR person such as yourself, will weather the storm a lot better than one whose reputation was already in the dumps. Not to mention, when you screw up (and you will), a good reputation will help save your own skin.

PR is not just about outward appearances or perception. Many people are unaware of this, but a lot of good PR also benefits a company's internal situation. When things are going south, employees start dusting off their resumes and looking for opportunities to jump the sinking ship. As a PR person, part of your job in managing the reputation of your client will be to raise the morale of the troops in the process. If they sense that things are turning around, that the perception of their company is changing, they may not be so keen on taking their talents elsewhere. Sometimes this is the most important contribution you can make to a business client. What good is securing the best lunch table in the cafeteria if there's no one there to sit with you?

PR Matters

Potential clients will often tell you that they don't need PR services. After all, they never do anything wrong and they never get into any sticky situations. They have totally got the public behind them, and it will be like that forever. It just so happened that a popular media outlet wrote about them once, and therefore, they're untouchable, everybody loves them, and they are in for a never-ending period of "organic growth." They couldn't be more wrong.

First of all, from a purely logistical perspective, there are just not enough hours in the day for your client to do a proper job of handling their own PR. A client can't pitch everybody, monitor the media, and manage their reputation while also staying focused on their core business. They wish they could. They may even think that they could. But that's because they've never done the job of a PR firm. Ultimately, you are the one with the contacts and expertise, and that will bring more results in a lot less time.

The client also doesn't realize that reading, researching, following, tweeting, absorbing, and understanding everything about themselves, their competitors, and their industry is an arduous task that is incredibly vulnerable to personal bias. Can you ever expect someone invested in their own success and the failure of their competitors to evaluate either of them objectively? Of course not. Besides, if your clients are doing their job correctly, they will not have the time to do all of this.

Meanwhile, it's your job to live and breathe everything about your client and the space they are competing in.

You're Not the First, But You Are the Freshest

When you start out in PR, you will have to accept a couple things.

1. You're not going to change the world.

2. No one is going to think your client is the Second Coming of Christ.

Unless your own overinflated narcissistic tendencies need to be knocked down a peg or ten, don't let this get you down. Everybody who decides to work in PR must realize this at some point. The world of PR, of reputation management, did not begin and end with your arrival on the scene. You do not hold the keys to the kingdom. So don't expect people to toss rose petals at your feet and chart you a path to the corner office.

That does not mean, however, that you are any less valuable than the older members of your team. Why? Because you have something they don't: a fresh perspective. As a newcomer to PR, your view of the business is free of experience (I mean that in the best way) and bias. To you, all things are possible. You aren't trapped by tradition or practices that make no sense because "this is how it's always been done." Why is this important? Because stupid ideas can come from anywhere. And if someone with standing and prestige comes up with a harebrained scheme to get publicity for the client, it can be disastrous if there isn't someone there to say, "Wait a minute." With a fresh perspective, you are more capable of seeing the chinks in the armor. At this point, on the public relations spectrum, you are still closer to "public" than to "relations," so you can provide critical insight about how this publicity scheme might be perceived by the people it's targeting. That is incredibly valuable.

Here's an example of what I mean by "fresh perspective": word-of-mouth advertising is still just as effective (that is to say, the *most* effective) as it has always been. If you hear about a restaurant from a friend, you're more likely to try it than if you heard a radio spot, watched a TV commercial, or saw a billboard for it. Your friend's description and enthusiastic rundown—what he ate, what the ambience and service was like, if the wait staff were attractive—might first only compel you to look for reviews on Yelp to be sure, but make no mistake, it was your friend's pitch (which is all it is, really) that got you in the door.

There are PR and marketing "gurus" with more experience than you who will disagree with this assessment vehemently. They will talk all kinds of shit about "social" and "engagement" and "authenticity" as the end-all, be-all, like that's an actual strategy. The reason they do this is because they have no clue what else to say and they are either trying desperately to climb up the corporate ladder or trying desperately to not get knocked off. They saw that Conan O'Brien has like a gazillion Twitter followers or they went to a conference all about social media and learned about hashtags for the first time, or the client is desperate to build up their social presence. Whichever one is truer, these gurus are convinced that trying to sound like a big shot is the way to get the job done. Fuck them. They're wrong.

Go with Your Gut

Think about all those silly stunts like the Janet Jackson "Nipplegate" scandal. The people who came up with that scheme were most likely established "gurus" telling executives what they wanted to hear—that they could be hip and cool by doing something edgy. We all know how that turned out. It was an unmitigated disaster for all parties. A lot of PR people got very rich trying to manage that situation and the reputations of everyone involved. And you know what? I bet there was someone like you, somebody new and inexperienced but with much better judgment than everyone else, who knew it was a shitty idea but didn't have the courage to speak up for what they believed in. As a new PR person, you can and should use your gut instincts to judge the validity of a solution, rather than just get caught up in current trends and the groupthink that others succumb to when they're tired of doing the work.

I'm not suggesting that you become a Luddite—technology will be your best friend in this gig—but you can and will succeed by adhering to tried-and-true methods. One is to trust your gut. Your instincts have been honed by Our Creator, or Evolution (or both—I'm not here to pass metaphysical judgment), over millennia to become effective tools for judging situations and outcomes. Do not ignore them. They are right most of the time.

The Pitch

The second tool you have in your arsenal will also never become obsolete. That tool is The Pitch. The Pitch is the story you want to tell about your client. Our computers and our phones and even our language may change, but what doesn't ever change is the way that people relate to each other, through the words we use and the stories we tell. Pitching is simply learning how words relate to people—what makes sense in a particular moment, what connects to a person and their own personal story versus what makes somebody walk away and wish you were dead.

Take Lance Armstrong. He had what we call a great reputation. It was built on years of achievement and amazing PR. He wasn't just a champion cyclist, he was a cancer survivor who used hard work and indomitable spirit to overcome perhaps life's greatest obstacle and touch the lives of millions across the world. That was the Lance Armstrong Story—The Pitch on Lance—and it connected. He was sponsored by some of the biggest brands in the world: Nike, Anheuser-Busch, Trek, Oakley. He was an American icon.

Yet over the last few years, members of the media, ex-teammates, former competitors, an entire sporting federation, and federal investigators have tried to bring Lance Armstrong down. They've subpoenaed him and his closest associates, they've threatened him, they've banished him, they've stripped away his medals and titles and yellow jerseys. They've done everything short of strip him naked, tar and feather him, and flog him in the town square (though don't think for a second they wouldn't if given the chance). Their efforts have taken their toll on Armstrong. He's lost nearly all of his corporate sponsorships, he's had to step away from the Livestrong Foundation (Nike ended their relationship with both Armstrong *and* Livestrong), and his Q Score has bottomed out to Kardashian-esque levels.

So what happened? Your first instinct is probably to say, "He cheated! He doped and used performance-enhancing drugs and lied about it and got caught." Wrong. While those are true facts, they are not the issue. Dozens of athletes have done the same thing and nearly all of them rebounded quickly. The problem is that Lance and his PR team lost control of the story. A notoriously tough nut to crack, Armstrong let pride and vanity get in the way. His PR team allowed him to let those things get in the way. They didn't adequately manage him or the situation. The result was a narrative they couldn't control and a story they couldn't spin.

There is nothing more human (or American) than a prideful liar who has worked his whole life to get to where he is and will do anything to protect himself once he gets there. And yet the irony is no one will consciously connect their personal story to it. They will turn around and walk away. Just as they have with Lance Armstrong. The Pitch falls on deaf ears.

Connection

When you can create an image of a company or a person that is lovable and desirable, you are telling the audience that, by doing business with that company or individual, they too can be lovable and desirable. Their lives can be better if they use this company's widget or wear this individual's personal fragrance. Good PR creates that connection of possibility between your clients and their customers.

This is part of a very basic idea: Humans crave connection. We want to live in the world with others who are just like us, whose needs and wants are so similar to ours that we put aside our superficial differences. We want to connect because it makes our lives better; it makes our lives feel more valuable. It doesn't matter if that connection is with a person, or a device, or a company.

Presidential campaigns are great at this. Those catchy slogans on yard signs and bumper stickers are designed to encourage and inspire a connection with one candidate, while also breaking down the connection with the candidate from the opposite party. Do you remember Barack Obama's "Yes We Can" slogan from the 2008 presidential campaign? Of course you do. Notice, it's "Yes WE Can" not "Yes *You* Can." WE, not *you*. WE is an us—a you and a me—connected by our "can"-ness. The slogan does double duty though. It also implies the converse of its literal message. If you don't support Obama, then you are not one of *us*—you are not WE—you are one of *them*. And they are bound by their "can't"-ness.

The beauty of that slogan is its inclusivity. Inclusivity is attractive—literally and figuratively—and creates connection. When voters feel that a candidate is speaking not just to them, but for them and with them, they are more likely to select that candidate. In PR-land, their pitch would be "You see these things I believe in? You believe in them too. They make sense to you! Because I'm just like you. I'm your guy."

Beyond the individual connection, there is also the collective connection—that innate need to be part of a group. We buy clothing that matches what our friends wear or that we feel will make us more appealing to those people we think we want to be friends with. We develop common interests with our friends beyond our own personal tastes because we want to belong to a group or to strengthen that preexisting connection. Just because Apple puts an 'I' in front of all their handheld and mobile products doesn't mean they are selling individual connection. The iPhone, the iPod, the iPad. Those are not individual products being sold to individual consumers. They are a lifestyle, a culture, an ecosystem. And you either get that—along with admission to the Apple Fanboy Collective—or you don't. All of Apple's marketing and PR supports that notion of culture and collective connection. They get it. Which is part of the reason they are the world's second-largest company by value.

Keep in mind that this desire for collective connection is distinct from peer pressure. Peer pressure is about *which* group to join. Collective connection is simply about the desire to join *a* group. We are social animals; that is where this need to belong comes from. A successful PR program capitalizes on and speaks to this longing.

If you create a campaign that shows how an individual has overcome adversity and bettered himself or herself in the process, who CAN'T resonate with that? Everybody wants to be better than they already are. Everyone wants to be a part of that group who lost 50 lbs. with Subway sandwiches like Jared, who found the love of their life with eHarmony, who "just do it" like Mike. We can connect with that aspect of these stores, because the triumphant and aspirational message makes us feel like anything is possible. Even if we are uncomfortable with the fact that right now, as we watch their commercials or see their billboards, we are overweight, alone, and unaccomplished, we've connected because we've found an element of fragility and humanity in public figures who seemed at times to be superhuman. That is connection, *par excellence*.

The "Cool" Factor

We've already established that reputation is the key to success for you and your client. Not only can a person or a company with a good reputation weather just about anything, they get the added benefit of being perceived as someone who is worth listening to. Their opinions—and therefore their products—have value. They have something to offer that others may not, and they end up getting noticed for all the right reasons. Then, the more highly others think of your client, the cooler they become.

Even if they're not actually Hollywood-cool or athlete-cool, they can still be cool in their niche. They might have an awesome Twitter account. They might have a successful blog that everybody reads that buoys them and their business. Maybe they designed a killer app, or they give away a bunch of cool stuff for free, or they fight for causes they believe in even when the cameras aren't rolling. Or maybe they just have really cool products. These are the sorts of things that give you an "in" with your target audience. When you play that right from the PR side, people eventually begin to think everything you do is cool. Steve Jobs was a creative and managerial tyrant who experimented wildly (and dangerously) with his diet, often only eating a single type of fruit for weeks at a time. And people were okay with that. They thought it was cool, because he made the iPhone, and the iPhone was fucking cool! It's like the transitive property of coolness.

Here's a great example about how the "cool factor" can make even the most mundane things seem like amazing acts of awesomeness:

One evening, I was dragged to a Dave Matthews Band concert, despite my fervent protests. It ended up being a very illustrative display of how the power of "cool" can alter people's perceptions. In between songs, Dave Matthews began to tune his guitar while performing. Normally you'd think, "Hey, I'm paying $120 for these tickets, play some damn songs! Don't you have roadies and guitar techs whose job this is?" But no, not with Dave. Dave's cool like that. He wasn't playing any music or singing, mind you. All he was doing was tuning his instrument. And the crowd went absolutely crazy. This was not an accident.

Dave Matthews and his PR machine have spent years cultivating his reputation and building his cool factor within his audience so that things like this little tuning interlude were just as cool. Lo and behold, the audience ended up going wild, like he was Hendrix playing "The Star Spangled Banner" at Woodstock. I don't think Dave Matthews is cool, but hey, I'm not his target audience. Those other people, the ones who have been following the DMB for years, they are his target audience, and they think he's as cool as an ocean breeze. Their opinion is the only one that matters.

The Malleability of Reputation

A good reputation is clearly instrumental in securing your client's financial future. The better the reputation, the more jobs they get or products they sell, the more money they make. Jessica Alba is a great example, on the other hand, of how a good reputation can help more than just the bottom line. A good reputation can be malleable and create flexibility in your client's future.

Alba has been a successful actress, model, and sex symbol for years. In 2001, at the age of twenty, she was the winner of the Maxim Hot 100. Everyone loved her. Women thought she was cute, men thought she was sexy, kids admired her. She's been nominated for a bunch of People's Choice and Kids' Choice awards. She never took any controversial movie roles, she played to her strengths, and she avoided all the typical pitfalls of young celebrities even going so far as to maintain strict "no-nudity" clauses in her contracts and sue Playboy for putting her on their cover without her permission. In 2008, at twenty-seven years old, she got married and had a baby.

Around this time, Alba started getting more openly involved in public service; working with children's charities, human rights groups, environmental and wildlife activists. Other celebrities might have taken a hit for this pivot away from what is expected of a Hollywood starlette. Not Alba. She has parlayed her acting and modeling career into a successful philanthropic and entrepreneurial career. She's no longer a sex symbol first and foremost, but a hard-working mom with a social conscience. And we know this because of some well-executed PR (who do you think spread the story about her putting up posters of great white sharks in Oklahoma City back in 2009??) and some strategic advertising deals.

Now, Jessica Alba is the woman behind The Honest Company (an eco-friendly hygiene product company) and one of the faces of Windows Phone. She's the hard-working technological mom, not just someone whose bikini posters teenaged boys hang on their bedroom walls. If she keeps this up, she's set for life, no matter which direction she wants to take.

The downside of reputation malleability, of course, is that having a good reputation today doesn't mean it will always stay that way. There are so many ways in which a reputation can be sullied that it becomes almost impossible to list the different PR nightmares you'll face over the course of your career.

People have ruined their reputations in all kinds of ways. They say something they shouldn't have (Paula Deen). They don't say something they should have (Lance Armstrong). They expose something they shouldn't have, be it emotional (Mel Gibson) or physical (Janet Jackson). They are too aggressive or too passive (Joe Paterno). Too loud or too quiet. Too radical or too copycat. Hell, almost anything can tarnish a client's reputation with a particular audience given the right circumstances.

What you need to take away from this exercise is that you need to understand expectations—not just how to set them for your client, but how to deliver on them. You need to know the audience and understand what they expect from your client. That means you need to be right there, embedded in the audience. Play their games, listen to their music, use the apps they designed. Audiences need to feel like the person you are asking them to invest in is on the same page as them.

That doesn't mean you won't piss somebody off—it's inevitable—but in the beginning of a PR campaign, you need to reach out to and please as many people in your target market as possible. Your audience will do all the heavy lifting, don't worry. They are the ones seeking connection, looking to feel connected to your client. All you have to do is make as much of your client accessible and connectable as possible. Doing so will result in connection, which in turn creates your client's reputation. And that is good PR. Now, your client might not be comfortable being so open and accessible. That's understandable. You get them through that by explaining that it's only for a finite period of time, until they've established the reputation they hired you to help create. After your client is solidly a part of their audience, then maybe their reputation can withstand some turmoil and a little withdrawal. But not until then.

Of course there is such a thing as too much access, too much sharing. There will be things about your client that you know will not go over well with your intended audience. Sometimes, you can avoid discussing them if they are irrelevant to your pitch. Details like religion, politics, sexual orientation, and other sensitive but personal matters fall under this category. If you are pitching a new book about Ignatius Loyola to a Catholic newspaper, you don't have to mention that the author, a noted theological scholar, is gay.

As a PR person, this is an easy concept to grasp. It is much harder to beat this into the brains of your clients, who view these details as part of their identity. Just ask whoever handled PR for the Dixie Chicks back in 2003 when they kicked off a world tour in London by railing against the Iraq War and stating that they were ashamed President George W. Bush was from their home state of Texas. Putting aside your political beliefs for a second, strictly as a PR person, you know that for an all-female country music act from Texas, less than two years after 9/11, with technology and media what it is, to say something like that publicly is an unmitigated disaster. Unfortunately, no one on the Dixie Chicks' PR team told the Dixie Chicks. Have you heard the new Dixie Chicks album recently? Of course you haven't. No one has. They went on "hiatus" in 2008.

The Dixie Chicks situation was preventable. Sometimes there are those things that everyone is going to find out about, whether you like it or not, even though (and sometimes precisely because) it runs counter to your interests. Sex tapes, DUI arrests, child custody and divorce proceedings, lawsuits. You need to deal with these things by doing some damage control. We'll discuss that later on in the book—just know that it's one of those things you're going to learn about on the job—and it may not be pretty.

The Consequences of a Mistake

When you're with your friends and you mess something up, they're going to forgive you pretty quickly. They won't think twice about the fact that you're human and that, like all humans, you make mistakes. But when someone is trying to build a reputation with a larger audience, they have to be on their best behavior. They don't just have to appear likeable—they need to be practically perfect.

Modern audiences are notoriously fickle. With the help of the media, they've made an art form out of building people up only to knock them down just as quickly. Given the chance, they will find something wrong with your client and they will pounce on it. All of a sudden, your client will be under the spotlight for their blunder, whether real or imagined. You need to make amends, and fast, lest your client get written off completely.

Today, even the smallest mistake or misstep can spiral into disaster. Hell, you may even have to deal with a crisis that originated from distorted information or outright lies, which were spread via shoddy reporting and unscrupulous bloggers. It's an absolute nightmare scenario, but one that is all too common in the Internet era. Today's media takes a cavalier approach to validating their sources. Bloggers don't always care if what they're saying is true, so long as it garners attention. Some will even pay for "information," prioritizing their own web traffic over accuracy or journalistic ethics. Reporters at traditional newspapers and magazines are generally more scrupulous, but even then, most reporters use blogs and even Wikipedia as source material. To say that either of these websites are paragons of accuracy is laughable. There will always be vested interests out there that can manipulate Wikipedia, blogs, and social media for their benefit, and the people doing this are well aware of what the consequences of this sabotage can be.

Yes, it's always possible for a post to be taken down or a correction to be made, but it might still be too late. Corrections, retractions, and stealth edits tend to escape the attention span of the Internet, meaning that you are left with a mess that looks impossible to clean up. You'll just have to make things as right as possible without being a dick to somebody who may have written or talked about your client in good faith, but had bad information. A trained professional such as yourself will be your client's best resource in situations like this. Think of yourself as the guardian of their precious reputation, the caretaker of their connections, and the keeper of their house (read: janitor).

A Final Note on Failure

I wish that the advice I impart on you could guarantee you a career free of failures or mistakes, but I can't. Failure is a part of our existence, and in PR especially, the situations leading up to it can be out of your control. You can pitch and network and tweet whatever message or story you want, after doing careful research to make sure it hits all the right notes and doesn't piss anyone off. But it's not always about what you do. In the end, it's up to your audience, the people you target with your pitches. If they don't take well to them, then you're fucked. You'll have a problem on your hands and you'll need to fix it, yesterday. That scenario is going to happen to you at some point, and you won't be able to do a thing about it. Does that prospect scare you at all?

No? Then good. Keep reading. You might just be cut out for a career in PR. Leave the open bars and movie stars to the amateurs.

the
first year
sucks

I originally was meant to start my first PR job in New York on October 1, leaving my post at *PC Zone* after just one year. As I celebrated my great move with some friends at a local pub, I received a message from my future boss telling me that I was "needed now." It was September 15. I responded, kindly and slightly drunk, that I had a life in England and that moving halfway across the world in such a short timeframe just wasn't possible. His response was terse, angry, and somewhat unhinged. He claimed that I didn't have it in me to do PR, that my heart wasn't in it, and the job was gone unless I was there the next day. He literally wanted me to materialize within the next twenty-four hours. I suggested a slightly more reasonable timeframe—one week. He was less than enthusiastic but he ultimately agreed and told me that he "appreciated the effort."

I acted as if I was eager and enthusiastic about accelerating the pace of my move; after all, I had earned this job after a long, hard fight. Deep down, I felt rushed and despondent—I had to shut down my life in the space of a few hours, and it hurt. I forwarded the emails to my

Dad, who said he was behind me either way (which I suppose he was, if you considered the plane ride). I ended up hopping on a plane, pulling off an entire transatlantic move in the space of seven days. It was horrible. I burned through a great deal of money simply buying the plane tickets and booking a hotel (which was cramped and awful), let alone meals for the first few days. I would end up not being paid for a month, due to an accounting error and not having a social security number. I found an apartment in just three days (an impossibly short time in Manhattan) but only because I had to.

The walls at my first workplace were an off-beige, the kind you'd expect to see in a rundown hospital or old person's home. The ceilings were low. The front-desk lady greeted me with the kind of saccharine friendliness that only comes from someone who has forced it so much they now hate every single human life that crosses their path. I was marched through the halls into a tiny little cubicle with no window, to exactly the same spot I had interviewed in—one that I thought was reserved purely for candidates so that they could be isolated during the job interview process. I was wrong. This was where I lived. A girl sat opposite me—I say that, but in reality she was behind a flimsy grey cubicle wall—and spoke in a forcefully happy voice about developing countries and payment methods and other nonsense. I was not sure what was going on. Was this all a joke? What was I doing? I got "introduced" via email to my new clients, none of which were big, or even medium, or even "good."

Within a few days I'd see three people frog-marched out of the office, fired. I'd be shouted at for wearing the wrong kind of shoes. I'd be told that I formatted a document wrong (the wrong bullet-point style) and threatened with being fired.

Fast forward two weeks, and I was given my first pitching assignment. An education company, something I'd come to know as a "startup," a word I hadn't heard before. I had an Excel document of different reporters' names, and I was told to "pitch them." I had no idea what the hell that meant. My manager stared at me blankly and said that I had to get them to write stories about the client. I smiled and was confident in everything that had been said to me—this was a job I'd love, I'd be good at and one that would sustain me in my crazed New York City lifestyle. I also had the perverse faith in this firm because it represented an author I was fond of. Surely they wouldn't steer me wrong.

I picked up the phone, as I had thousands of times as a journalist, and called an education reporter from a long list of education reporters.

"Hi, I'm Ed Zitron from <firm>, I represent <Client>,—" I began, launching into a nervous tirade about an algebra challenge. The guy cut in. "No, no, no," he said, and I heard the click and slam of a reporter hanging up on me. With that, I realized that I was not important. After a few more calls, I'd come to realize that phone calls have become today's version of the door-to-door salesman. I was a nuisance. So I started emailing people and pretending to be on the phone. My manager would walk past my cubicle and I'd frantically pick up my phone and start blabbering about mobile payments and she'd nod confidently. My results improved slightly as I focused more and more on making emails that A) stood out and B) weren't awful to read.

After a few months' time, I had my performance review, where I'd be told my writing was horrible, my attitude was "bad," and I was hanging by a thread. The only reason I hadn't been fired was that I had developed a little bit of skill at pitching reporters. I had placed a few stories but my pitches were still awful, rambling monstrosities. Despite that, people answered my emails. I danced the very common dance in a PR firm beset by a consistently rotating client base—handling bureaucratic tasks like formatting an agenda properly while producing just enough results to avoid being punted out of the building.

I would cry a little, every so often, in the bathroom, which was the only place where you could escape the constant surveillance of your bosses. Sometimes I'd be in there for over an hour. I gained a twitchiness that would shut off my monitor the moment I heard footsteps, and I'd learn to keep my hand on my cellphone and anything else on my desk, lest it get cleaned away, taken by a "curious" manager who was intent on snooping through it. It wasn't quite as totalitarian as I make it sound, but the overall feeling was one of abject fear—the fear of losing one's job, one's livelihood, one's dignity—and it governed much of my first year in the PR business.

....

Blood, Sweat, Tears

With all of the energy and enthusiasm you have right now for PR, there's a truism that bears repeating; it's hard work. If it wasn't hard work, everyone would be doing it—and everyone would be doing it well, making lots of money, living in big houses, and shopping at Saks Fifth Avenue. But not everyone is destined for these trappings, precisely because they are rewards for hard work; for your blood, sweat, and tears. And there will be lots of tears, from losing clients, from your first (and last) chewing-out by your boss, from just straight-up not being able to produce results…and more. If you're okay with that, and you've decided that a job in PR is the way you want to get all those designer clothes and fancy jewelry, then the best thing you can do is forget about them, for a long time. Don't listen to all those fools in Hugo Boss suits trying to blow smoke up your ass who haven't actually done client work in the last five years. Instead, find a comfortable chair and plant your butt firmly in it. Because it's time to get to work.

The Buffer & The Bullhorn

Think about how PR is applicable to the world around you. You can look nearly anywhere in the media today to see examples of how PR would be helpful in negotiating difficult situations. You can see where it's being utilized properly and where it needs to be implemented. Even if you've never done this sort of work before, you probably have an intuitive understanding of the field. Yes, PR is about managing reputations for your client, but there is another element to it as well, one that will have more relevance to your day-to-day duties.

You need to become both the buffer and the bullhorn between the client and the public. As the buffer, you will help clients keep their private lives private. You will often be all that stands between private and public, between privacy and publicity, when fans or the media start sniffing around. Sometimes this will be at odds with your other role as the bullhorn, where you will need to become the voice and the sole conduit for audiences to find out what's really happening with your client—not the blogs, or the media, or Internet forums. This applies especially for any media that wants to know more about your client or discuss them in any way that may not be in your client's best interest. That is when you are both buffer and bullhorn at the same time. Just remember: your goal is to be the exclusive source for all information on your client. The *type* of information will help you determine when to be the buffer and when to be the bullhorn.

Don't Be Amazing, Be Effective

Not long ago, I had lunch with an old friend who worked in government and was in charge of immigration. He was thoroughly annoyed that even in an enormous pool of applicants competing for a scarce number of jobs, he couldn't find any qualified applicants—and this was in a pool that contained a number of PhDs.

I couldn't help but laugh at his problem. We hear all about how companies like Google ask for your school transcripts and make applicants jump through mental hoops just to prove how intelligent they are. He had the opposite problem.

"I don't need smart. These PhDs live in their own world. They're useless to me," he said. "They can't interact, they can't finish anything on time, they're stuck in their academic fantasyland. I need capable. I need effective."

Remember this at all times. You need to be effective, and that means getting results for your client. No one cares how smart or witty or avant-garde or well connected you are if you can't get the job done. Bear in mind, I am not saying you have to suppress your personality or character at work, nor am I suggesting you should refrain from using any established contacts you have to help you out—provided they are relevant and useful. What I am saying is that you need to be the person who is focused on doing things for the client, with a clear outcome in mind. This period, your first year, is about making the client look really good, not making your career look promising. Do not forget that. Besides, you can't have the latter without the former.

The Basics of Agency Life

I could write an entire book about the ins and outs of agency life, the pitfalls and all the tricks, but it really all boils down to this.

Day Zero. You will get your HR orientation package, IT will set up your new computer, and you will be assigned a cubicle and the restroom security code (don't forget this one!). You'll start off probably as an Account Coordinator or an Account Executive. It's a great title to have, because when your Grandma tells everyone what you do, it sounds important. But make no mistake, you're only one step above the mailroom. You will be given no training. Expect to get an Excel spreadsheet with a list of reporter names and a bunch of email addresses and phone numbers. You will be told to make coverage happen. There will be some writing involved, but the pressure will be on you to pitch, pitch, and pitch some more. Don't know how to pitch? Don't worry. That's why you bought this book.

There will be pressure from all levels above you—from Account Executives, Directors, Managers, VPs, General Managers, and all sorts of other weird titles. These people will present your results to the client. And to make matters worse, they will not only take credit for the good work you do, but they'll also blame you when things go wrong. It's a shitty racket. It's corporate hazing, but it's no different than in any other industry. Investment bankers on Wall Street start out in the exact same situation; on call at 10 p.m. on a Friday in case their boss wants a cheeseburger delivered to their desk. The world's best chefs peeled potatoes and chopped carrots until their hands bled before they were ever allowed to cook anything of consequence. Everybody goes through it. The only difference is the exact shape and form of the hell you have to survive. But survive it, and eventually you'll be tasked with more exciting and challenging tasks like drumming up new business.

Making Connections

When you first started dating, you probably chose some less than ideal people to meet for coffee or a movie. At first, they may have swept you off your feet. But then you noticed that certain something that put you off. Maybe they're selfish or inconsiderate. Maybe they make promises they can't keep and never do what they say they're going to do. Networking can be similar. You might be charmed by someone initially, but when it comes time to get something accomplished, they don't come through for you. It's up to you to keep your network useful and valuable, to make sure your relationships are reciprocal and worth your time and investment.

Later on, we'll cover networking in greater detail, but it's important enough that I'm going to discuss it here as well. The most important takeaway is that networking is a continuous process that can take months, or even years, to produce something of value for your work. **Do not expect immediate results.** In fact, your best contacts will probably not provide you with anything tangible for a long time. But when you look back on it, you'll realize that every cup of coffee you bought them or question you asked was just one step on the way to the opportunity that sits in front of you right now. You are here to *connect* with people—that is your job, not find people to use for your own ends.

Getting to know your contacts on a personal level is a great way to make friends out of the people—like bloggers and journalists—who cover the industry. Let them be the one to bring up your field or your client. It will make you appear human, rather than just another hungry flack looking to get a story planted. Some of these people may end up going to your wedding, your kids' bar mitzvah, or even your funeral. The connections you make often cross over from your professional life into your personal life. Don't forget that.

Even though you're going to be busy with your own PR tasks, you also need to be available to others as well. You need to be ready to help the people in your network when they need it, or else you're not fulfilling your end of the bargain in the networking relationship, which is to be of value to your contacts in exchange for their own expertise and knowledge. You may not be able to offer your experience and wisdom at this point, but even something as simple as an introduction to somebody who may be of service to them can be a great help and will go a long way with your contacts and their estimation of you. It doesn't even have to be someone in PR or media. Recommending a great mechanic or a house painter can be more useful than introducing a contact to yet another app developer or artisanal cheese maker.

Say Goodbye to Your Life as You Know It

Even though you may have this grandiose image in your head of a glamorous life, full of parties and celebrities and beautiful people, your first year will look nothing at all like that. True, you might need to go to client events, but your first client probably isn't going to be with Mister or Miss Gorgeous Movie Starlet, so don't start shopping for Oscar gowns just yet.

Instead of thinking about the glitz and glamor, you need to maintain a constant focus on your work. In each moment, you should be thinking about them, researching them, and taking the appropriate action to keep their reputation golden. You should be going over your strategy, deciding if it still works, and making adjustments if needed. You should be talking to your client and seeing if there is more you can do that you haven't already done. You should know where they're fitting into their industry and how you can improve their situation. The more time you put into this process in the beginning, the more benefits your client will see, and the more benefits *you* will see in the end. Let's face it—someone who doesn't have a life because of his or her work does seem more serious about it to current and prospective clients. Learn how to focus and understand an industry early in your career—and your client relationship—and you will be able to learn new ones faster and more effectively later on.

Automating the Drudgery

Taking on a new client won't be the last time you do research on your client's reputation. You are going to do this every single day until you leave the business. Aside from pitching, keeping on top of what people say about your client is going to be the most important part of your job. You will have to read all kinds of articles, tweets, blogs, and news items about your client, and the forms in which they come to you will only continue to grow and change. But the key, as far as being a PR professional goes, is that they *come to you*, not that you waste time seeking them out. You can engineer things to do just that by taking advantage of current automating technologies. They will be your best friends early on, trust me.

Instead of doing daily Google searches (not that you should skip these), you can sign up for Google Alerts that will deliver links to your inbox, based on the keywords you select. You can receive the links as often as you like, and then you can respond to things that come up online immediately. You can use as many keywords as you like—the company name, the client name, etc. Yes, your email box will be flooded with results, but many won't be relevant. Use those irrelevant results to eliminate ineffective keywords and hone in on the valuable one. This will help you get efficient.

You also need to have access to all your client's accounts, whether it's a blog, or social media, or an email list, or a talking parrot. You need to be able to get into any of them at any time to see what's going on and what you may need to do in order to clean up a mess or seize an opportunity. This is a key part of being a good PR person, especially early on. At the very least, you need links to all of the places where your client's information might already be.

If you have access to all of these accounts, you'll want to turn on all of those notification features so you don't have to navigate to the sites repeatedly throughout the day. You can have notifications sent to your email inbox, your desktop (in certain cases), and your smartphone. This will help you keep track of what's going on, so you can respond appropriately.

Email

Once you've signed up for more email than you can handle, you'll need to find ways to keep track of all of the information flooding in. It's time to get organized before things get out of control. If you're using Gmail or a similar email program, then you can create folders for emails with the things you've found online, as well as the responses you may have generated.

The Cloud

You may also want to invest in a cloud storage option (e.g. Google Drive, Dropbox, etc.) so you can store your work and your responses in a safe place that can be accessed by the client at any time. This is a place where you can save PDFs of the things you have done and the web pages where not-so-nice things have popped up.

Spreadsheets

Spreadsheets and Microsoft Excel will be your new best friend, so take some time to learn how to use them. Buying a book or tutorial program isn't a bad idea, and there may even be a course you can take at a community college to master it. If so, I highly recommend it, as it's a powerful organizational tool. Personally, I like to keep spreadsheets for different clients that outline the actions I've taken and what kind of response I've gotten. You can list the links to the pages where you found PR issues or opportunities for your client, and then also have a column for the ways you took action. This sheet can be submitted every week or every month to the client for review. This will help to quantify the work you've done and provide a way for you to follow up as needed. It's a small gesture that will go a long way for your own reputation.

Tracking

For your pitches, you can use an email tracking program—ToutApp is great as it tracks when a person reads or responds to your emails.

This will help you keep an eye on what emails and pitches are getting read. And ignored.

You will want to send these to your client to see if they are on board with what you are sending out in your pitch emails, or if they have any constructive feedback for you. The more you keep the process collaborative, especially in the beginning of your PR work, the more a client will trust you.

It also never hurts to read about the competition either. You want to know them as intimately as you would if they were paying you. Make note of when they are mentioned as well as when your client is mentioned. Competitive intelligence is key here. You must understand your industry, including more successful and better-looking adversaries. Reading things like magazines, trade journals, and the appropriate sections of the newspaper will give you a good overview of what's going on in your field of interest.

Forums: Where the Bodies Are Buried

If you want to hear what customers REALLY think, you need to meet them where they're going to be as honest as possible. That place is online forums.

Forums have become the hot spots for learning about the reputation of companies and of people in general. People on these message boards are talking about their unique needs, offering advice to other users, and demonstrating how a company's PR strategy is working. Or not. First of all, you'll need to sign up before you can post on them. If you're happy just to read the forums, many will let you review the posts without an account.

From there, you might want to start asking questions about what the users think about your client. Tread carefully, as the forum users are very savvy about your client's product and the industry as a whole. Every forum has its own distinct culture with inside jokes, well-known posters, and other subtle details. They can smell a rat almost immediately.

Reverb Communications (a PR firm), for example, piqued the interest of Internet users when comments for a client of theirs seemed a little too positive. It turned out that these users were Reverb staff, and by not disclosing that they were part of the company they were breaking the law. They eventually settled with the Federal Trade Commission—a big slap in the face for the client and a fat asterisk on every result Reverb's ever had. The irony? I really like Reverb. They just did a really stupid thing.

Your investigation will require some discretion and finesse. The best way to accomplish this is to read them for a while, get a handle on the culture and discourse (every forum is a little different), and then dive into posting. If you can, offer advice or experiences (real or imagined) on the boards, as this can help you seem like a real user and not just a collector of information. That way you're more than just another "shill" for your client. The more you go onto forums, the more you will notice that some people are doing the same things you will do in your PR role. Not everyone is looking for information. Some of them are such fans of your client—you'll sometimes hear them called "evangelizers"—that they'll advocate on your behalf for free.

Read Reviews

If you're not reading reviews, you're not doing your job. Look for reviews on blogs, on review sites, on Amazon, on Yelp, and all points in between. Don't just focus on professional critics either. Find out what real people think about the client and the company. Make a list of positive and negative comments, take note of what the public identity and brand already is, and then refer back to your notes from the client about how they actually want to be seen. That is the essence of balancing the message with the reputation in building your client's brand.

It's Not Just About Your Client

Yes, you know that this is all about your client, but a small bit of attention needs to be placed on you.

Since you're speaking up for your client, you need to be someone that people want to deal with as well. That means you need to conduct yourself professionally. You can't just show up for PR events late, and you can't say just anything on your personal Facebook page anymore and think people won't connect it to your job. People will be looking at you. Everything you do matters right now. When you begin to realize this, you can see how you need to be more measured and mature in your decisions and actions.

If you're not doing something for yourself and for your reputation, you're not doing anything for the reputation of your client. And while you might not have anything to do with your client outside of work, people will start to draw that connection if you give them the chance. If you earn yourself a bad reputation, then guess what, your client does too. They get to have the added "benefit" of being linked with your idiotic choices.

For example, there are plenty of reporters I've sassed over Twitter who now won't run stories with me. A dumb move on my part.

Everything that you do from the time you begin your PR career to the time you stop or get fired is about your client. That's it. If you wanted to have a life and you wanted to have people not notice you, then you've chosen the wrong line of work. Of course, you're not going to get the same sort of attention, but you are going to be a part of the reputation of your client, and that means you will draw the same scrutiny. It's the dark side of the halo effect.

The Case for Being Nice

Hollywood seems to have conjured up this idea that PR people need to be mean and sarcastic to the downtrodden and less-than-beautiful, because that's how you make fabulous people look and feel fabulous and wealthy. By their estimation, playing nice isn't the way to make things happen. Again, this is something that is only applicable in TV land.

That doesn't mean you need to be a pushover, but it does mean that you need to be as pleasant as possible in your interactions while also standing your ground. Use your manners. Treat others the way that you want to be treated. Count to ten before you respond to jerks.

When you're pleasant to others around you, it takes away a lot of the power from your enemies. First of all, they can't accuse you of being unkind to them. Second, being nice to people will make them more inclined to be nice to you, or even do a favor for you. The PR professional that is kind and pleasant may not stand out, but they won't be someone people will actively avoid.

Just as you need to be nice to everyone you work with and for, you also need to be nice to everyone who doesn't seem to matter in the moment. When you're out with your client, you need to tip well and say "please" and "thank you." You need to treat everyone around you like they are going to start talking about you the second you leave. Even though your client should be getting most of the attention, you will be garnering some of the attention too, so act accordingly. Be nice to the wait staff, the valet, and the coat check girl. People will be watching, especially the client.

As you get more experience, then you can be a bit more aggressive and demanding, maybe a little less kind. But for now, nice wins the day, especially because you are going to meet a ton of new people and there is no telling who will be friend and who will be foe.

Who You'll Meet

During your PR career, you'll be able to meet a number of professionals who are not only there to help you, but who can also teach you what you need to know about the industry. To make sure you're ready for all these new wonderful people, let's get to know them briefly. Like clients, there's no one-size-fits-all description, but this should be enough for you to use as a handy little field guide.

The Media

You will reach out to the media whenever you can or whenever it seems appropriate, depending on your clients. These might include people from the local news stations, newspapers, and other media outlets. They are a diverse bunch and not easily categorized. You will get to know them intimately just by the nature of your symbiotic relationship. Your job is to pitch stories; their job is to write stories.

News reporters will typically be on a tight deadline and you'll need to respond to them right away with a quote, a piece of information, or a confirmation of something they think they already know. You may work with them on longer stories, but usually their deadline is at the end of the work day.

Magazine reporters have longer lead times and will usually correspond with you multiple times about the same issue. Their pieces are longer, more in-depth, and better researched, but it can take them months to get published so you have to factor that into your client's PR strategy and timeline.

TV anchors will never get in touch with you. Sorry. If you want to pitch a story or a client for a guest appearance, you want to talk to the producer. Producers are the ones who set the agenda for TV news programs and radio shows. They're going to be your main point of contact. You may talk to TV reporters, but it will usually be on similar terms as a newspaper reporter. Make sure that before you pitch TV producers, you have watched their show and know the ins and outs of who it targets, what network they're on, who their competitors are, and any other details that are relevant (as if they are a client). TV producers are inundated with requests, so you better come prepared.

For example, the producer at Taking Stock with Pimm Fox at Bloomberg TV really likes me. Why? Because I know about the show. I know it's very different from Surveillance (a show more about the markets) and West (very Bay-area and more startup-focused). I know how Pimm's personality is different than other anchors. Furthermore, I also know that if I try to pitch them someone who's too small, they'll be upset.

Taking a step back, if I go to a completely new producer on, say, Fox Business, I need to make sure I've watched the show because if I pitch them someone so utterly, totally not fit for a show, they'll ignore my email. Conversely, if I nail the pitch because I know the show backwards and forwards and side-to-side, they'll be quite happy. They also might not even read my email, but that's a risk you take with every click.

Social Media Personalities

Even though you may never meet a social media personality in person, you can "meet" them by going online and interacting with them. The more you tweet at them, the more you share their Facebook statuses, the more of a bond you will have. You don't have to sit down for coffee to have a relationship anymore, not on the Internet. So make sure you know how to communicate in their language and the language of whichever medium they have built their personality on.

Bloggers

Closely related to social media personalities are those who blog about the industry and what's happening in it. The bloggers today are the leaders in PR for themselves and for things they care about—even if they're not getting paid.

They've spent time and energy building up audiences who are listening to them, and then they talk. These bloggers know how to gain trust from their followers, and they make sure they're not taking advantage of it. We could all stand to learn from them.

Of course, there are different kinds of bloggers. Your run-of-the-mill angry guy living in his mom's basement ranting about your client may not be worth engaging. Other independent bloggers may actually be superb journalists who can write, research, and edit with the best of them. They will be worth your time. You can use tools like QuantCast to check their legitimacy and see just how big of a blog they really have. I like to work with blogs that have 5,000 or more unique readers per month. If 5,000 people are interested in a topic and reading about it regularly, then the blogger is someone you should connect with.

Bloggers who write for established outlets like the *New York Times* and *Wall Street Journal* are just as reputable as any reporter, and even have editors overlooking their work to ensure accuracy. Bloggers at major, well-funded blogs are a mixed bag. Some of them care about accuracy, but the vast majority are content to publish first and verify later. This is how false information gets spread, and it can be a real pain in the ass to walk back or unwind. Unfortunately, it's the nature of the Internet.

Your Network

Along the way, you will also meet people who will help you get your client noticed in some way. They might not be the typical media sources either. What they are is a part of your network. One of my favorite people in the world is a guy who also writes a LinkedIn column—one that gets shittons of traffic. Start collecting numbers in your phone, pages in your address book, and any other contact info you can. Make a note about what they can provide to you and what you may be able to offer them in return. Keep your network alive as the more they are connected with you, the more they might be able to put you in touch with even more important people.

Other PR People

While you may not begin your PR career with a lot of connections, you want to start reaching out to other PR agencies and companies as soon as it makes sense for you. In doing so, you can help share resources and you can find out what others are doing for their clients.

Even though you might wince at the idea of sharing your resources, remember that not all PR companies want to work with everyone. That might be YOUR motto right now, but it's not what everyone is doing.

Marketing People

While the ad department may not put themselves out there as having PR capabilities, they are just as integral to your client's PR efforts as you are. Start learning more about the marketing forces in your area today and how they relate to your client's industry. This can help you find out what you're doing wrong or what these people might be able to do for you down the road. Marketing and PR may be distinct fields, but they are intimately related and there are many lessons to be learned where they intersect.

The Competition

You can also rely on your competition for the help you need in your PR journey. Not only can they show you good examples of PR, when they're kicking your client's ass, but they can show you what not to do when you're kicking theirs. Even though they may not realize it, every time your competition tries something, and you're watching, you are getting a window into their strategy. The best part is, you don't need to ask them a single question. Just look at what they're doing. Be ready to hand out your card to anyone you might connect with about PR stuff in the future. These connections will become more valuable than you realize.

Making Mistakes and Learning from Them

In the beginning of your PR career, you will constantly be learning and adapting. You will find out that certain strategies are highly effective in certain situations, while others are worse than useless. You will get your feelings hurt when your boss or your client reams you for a mistake you made. You will screw up and fail. You will feel dizzying highs when you succeed.

When things go wrong, you really only have a few options:

1. Quit.

2. Hide under your covers.

3. Learn from the mistakes.

Even though #1 and #2 might seem preferable, what separates the professional from the amateur is that the professional remembers their errors, takes responsibility, and then doubles down on their efforts to do better next time. As a rookie, you will have a hard time predicting how the audience will react to your PR tactics. Only with experience will you be able to predict the audience's responses for future clients. Just remember to be honest about what happened and self-critical if necessary. If someone on your team did it, that's fine too—but make sure to own up to it.

In a twisted way, you should rejoice when you make an error, because you'll learn a lot more from your screwups than from your successes.

Remember that there is no one-size-fits-all strategy, and this is all an experiment to see what works and what doesn't at a particular place in time. You will have to constantly revamp and refine your strategies based on the results you get. You might find that you are able to manage the PR needs of one client with constant monitoring, while another requires minimal attention. What can be helpful is to write down all of the things you do and why you chose to do them in the first place. Yes, you need to keep a journal. It sounds lame, but it is an extraordinarily useful resource. When you do this, you'll have a strategy book that allows you to review your past moves—both successes and failures—which will hopefully give you some insight for the future.

Are You the Right Person for the Job?

At some point or another in your first year of PR, you will ask yourself if you are the right person for the job. You will question why you ever wanted to get into a business filled with difficult strategies and impossible decisions. These periods of doubt and questioning are normal, even healthy.

If you manage to get past this mini existential crisis, you'll come out ahead. Why? Because most people give up. Some get scared off after their first mistake. They're not willing to push through the "dips" in their career, which is absolutely essential for success in PR. I knew an amazingly talented guy in PR—great at media relations but a terribly fluffy writer with a caustic personality. When he'd constantly butt heads with supervisors over his ideas (some good, some bad), he'd be totally unable to take the criticism. As a result, in his eventual firing, he never went back into PR. A loss for the industry, a loss for him.

Many middle managers think that PR is about appearance and perfection. For them, looking bad or screwing up is a fatal error and the end of their world.

To be perfectly honest, I'd question whether those people wanted to be in PR in the first place. After all, if you go into any job thinking you'll be perfect, then you're dangerously naïve or woefully overestimating yourself. There isn't one professional out there, in a career they can stomach, who hasn't made some mistake at some point.

What a lot of new PR people don't realize when they're first starting out is that few people get what public relations is. With that in mind, you need to remember that those around you already consider you a pro. Even if you never took a PR course or reached out to anyone for a favor, clients already see you as a professional. It's on your business card, and your LinkedIn profile, and the other side of the @ symbol in your email address. The world says you are a PR professional. Now act like one.

I'd started working with Pando Networks (not to be confused with tech blog PandoDaily) at my second agency on a lark; they streamed game data using peer-to-peer technology. In essence, you'd download a game, and you'd share bits of it while you were playing it with those closest to you (or download from local peers). The result was a faster connection, even if your Internet wasn't particularly high end. We spent the first few months going back and forth over ideas, getting games media placements and generally having consistently more mundane conversations until one day when somebody mentioned "data."

"Big data" has become a new term for PR people to bastardize. It refers to having a lot of sources (over, say, a few thousand) and using said data to make elaborate claims about society. However, Pando Networks had millions of data points on download speeds across the world. At first blush, this wasn't that interesting until they broke down the data into city-by-city statements of kilobyte-per-second download speeds.

Robert, the CEO, was the kind of client who would try anything if there was a well-thought-out plan behind it. He let me commission an infographic, gave me full access to the data, and let me off the chain. A few weeks later, we had a national front-page story in the *New York Times*, coverage all over the tech and consumer press (on a local and national scale), and a consistent influx of media questions. It was PR heaven made reality and only happened because Robert and I sat down and talked a lot. We had a relationship that was built on talking regularly and sharing information on both sides that could make the business sing in the press.

··

Dealing with Clients

Working with clients is a lot like a romantic relationship. You can read *Cosmo* articles and jargon-filled books all you want, but there's no substitute for the experience of an actual partner. Without it, you will have an incredibly difficult time building a stable, loving relationship based on important things like trust and respect.

PR isn't much different. You and the client have found each other and are about to embark on a journey where you will both grow together, sharing positive and negative experiences while hopefully having some fun every now and then. You'll be approaching things from two completely different perspectives, but unlike a relationship, where it's up to both of you to compromise in order to make things work, in a PR-client relationship, the onus will be on you to make your partner (aka the client) happy.

That is not to say that this isn't a collaborative process, because it is. Their input is essential to a successful PR strategy, but it is by no means the end all, be all. You're the PR professional, not the client. In the end, you're going to have to be the dominant one when it comes to strategy and tactics. No "What do *you* want to do?" or "I don't care,

I'll do whatever." None of that. You wear the pants, unequivocally. This is where the comparison to romantic relationships ends.

You can take the lead with your client in a number of ways. The easiest way, I find, is to discuss what everyone else is doing. Talking about the PR campaigns of the competition can be a good way to jumpstart the discussion in the direction you want; whether it's highlighting bad campaigns you want to steer them away from or great ideas you want them to buy into. Even if they are enthusiastic about getting started on the whole thing, you always want to subtly lead the process. You want to be attentive to their needs while not letting their energy take control of the program.

From there, you can slowly finesse your way into finding out how the client wants to get involved with PR. Do they think their social media presence is lacking? What media outlets would they like to build relationships with? How do they perceive their own reputation, and is it where they want it to be? Be aware though, you can ask one hundred clients in very similar situations those same questions and you'll get one hundred wildly different answers. That's because there are different types of clients who will inevitably respond differently to the same set of facts. It's important to recognize and understand those client types.

The Client Archetypes

If you're like me and you slept through Classical Greek and Roman studies, then you probably missed the lecture on archetypes. An archetype is a basic, fundamental character type that exists in all forms of storytelling, whether books, plays, movies, or TV—the Reluctant Hero, the Damsel in Distress, the Wise Old Man, etc. They exist in art and literature, and they exist in PR as well. You will have to adapt to the subtleties and quirks of each client archetype, as quickly and as often as they pop up in your world. I've identified a few basic archetypes over the last five years that I will sketch out below to give you a head start.

The Ever-Shifting Client

One of the most "challenging" clients you will meet is the one that seems to have a new idea and a new business plan every two seconds. They will say that they're "adapting to the marketplace" or "pivoting to meet consumer demand," but really the core of their indecisiveness is the fact that they don't have a complete understanding of their business or their brand.

It's fine to have new ideas and to evolve, but when your client is constantly presenting new ideas and strategies that contradict previous ones, it can get a little problematic. When they change the rules and move the goal posts, it's almost impossible to tell if anything is working, there's almost no way to accurately measure success, and heaven forbid you try to ensure they're happy.

You will need to be firm with this client. If you aren't, it's a recipe for sleepless nights and pulling your hair out, all before their PR plan is even in place. Remember, they're just scared. They're not sure they've got it right, which leads to a bit of an identity crisis, which leads to panic and rash decisions when they're not seeing immediate results, even when those results are not your fault or your responsibility. Let them know that you want them to succeed and that sticking to one plan will be the best way to remain on the right path. What I like to do is make the client stick to a given plan that we have mutually agreed on for thirty days and let them see the results for themselves. Sometimes, this will be too short of a time frame (and feel free to alter these terms as necessary), but the point is to establish expectations; results are usually not immediate and they will have to understand this.

The "Whatever" Client

On the other end of the spectrum is the client that doesn't really care what you do. They'd rather just let you do your thing and then speak up if something goes wrong. Often this client is either someone who is new to their business or someone who has been around for a while and has achieved a certain amount of success. They just want to keep coasting and making money, but they still want to have their PR managed by a professional. You might ask yourself why they're even coming to you in the first place since they seem to have their act together. It's because they come from a world where it is commonly understood that a PR person is necessary for running a good, smart business, even though they have no idea why that is the case. That's why they'll just shrug their shoulders, nod, and write the check after you present the PR strategy that took hours and hours to create.

Don't be offended. Instead, get this client more engaged in what you are doing. Their apathy may be hard for you to break through initially, but this is where you have to turn on all your charm and cheer to help them understand that PR is a two-way street. Maybe you have some way of showing them tangible benefits they have not enjoyed with previous PR strategies (i.e., how much money they'll save or generate). How you do it is up to you. Just know that you cannot go it alone and wait for them to give you (negative) feedback. By then it's too late.

The Popular Client

As you get more experience and start to develop a reputation for being good at what you do, you are more likely to sign a client who is already popular with their audience. They will regale you with stories about

51

how successful they are, how great their reputation is, how awesome they are (or think they are).

The thing with a client like this is that they often think you can't do anything for them. They're the king of the world—what could you possibly tell them that they don't already know? And with a standard awareness campaign, they'd probably be right. Your efforts won't seem like they are changing anything. You need to start thinking about what they AREN'T doing, and then attack their PR strategy from that point of view.

You also want to start talking about their long-term strategy. It's great that they're successful now, but coasting on that will only lead to future complacency, laziness, and ruin. Sit down with them and discuss their goals and vision for the future. If they don't have them, then they may not be popular for very long. And then they'll really need you.

The Unreachable Client

The client that doesn't seem to be available can be the hardest to handle when you're new to the PR business. Even though they might be super excited at the start, they suddenly disappear. They don't answer your emails. They don't answer your calls. They don't give you any feedback and they don't have anything to add when there are problems.

This is going to drive you nuts if you let the client continue to act this way. Unlike the apathetic client, these types tend to think that they don't need to be involved.

You have to be the one who initiates contact with this client, and while this might take up a bit of your time, the client or your boss will never be able to say you aren't doing all that you can. Make it clear that you will not act on any strategies without their approval, and make sure that you have set appointments for getting in touch with them. If they continue to be elusive, you might want to stop working with them. The relationship won't be beneficial for anyone.

The Demanding Client

The demanding client is the one that all new PR people are afraid of, but this is actually one of the easier clients to deal with. At least they're engaged. They just don't care about how much work this puts on you. Or they might not completely trust you. Or they think because they're paying you, no matter what the fee is, that they own your time. Often, the demanding client is just scared that all of the work you're doing isn't going to pay off, so you may need to give them regular reports about what is happening with their reputation. Prove your awesomeness to them, soothe them, and they will slowly back down.

In any case, you need to set some boundaries so you don't get trampled on every time you talk. They need to understand the expectations of the working relationship—what constitutes extra work above and beyond your normal duties. Yes, you need to go to the wall for your client as a rule, but repeated "emergency" phone calls at 2 a.m. because "someone" forgot the password to their Twitter account will inevitably drive you to the edge of your sanity.

In the end, you have to decide if this is something you can handle. If it is, then just keep being clear about the plan that you mutually agreed upon. Eventually, they will back off and let you do your thing. Or they will fire you and make somebody else's life miserable.

The Flaky Client

If you take on a client who is flaky, that's when the real troubles can come.

They might be as sweet as can be, but they don't remember anything you told them and they're not available when you want them to be. Appointments are merely vague suggestions to them, and they won't be around when you need to talk to them about important matters.

The danger here is that you start losing respect for them. You might begin to feel like a parent to this childish client who needs a lot of handholding. Worse, they start to feel out of touch, like they don't know what they're doing. And your natural instinct is to feel like they're not worth your time. Don't fall into this trap. They might just be overwhelmed by the idea of success. Show them that you can be trusted and that you expect the same from them. Make them understand that you are on the same team, that your success is their success and vice versa.

Right now, you are aiming to be steady, stable and slightly conservative in your approach, so use these archetypal sketches as a guide. As you mature as a PR professional, you can get more daring and start taking risks. By then you can confidently assert that you know better, or at least that you know what you're doing.

No Client Is Perfect—And Neither Are You

When things go really bad is also the exact time that you'll have to keep a firm grip on both the media and your client. A client that's emotionally engaged with their product may try to directly engage with the reporter, or the blogger, and make a huge mistake. Take the recent controversy over the *New York Times* and their road test of the Tesla Model S electric car. After the *Times'* demo car ran out of juice, Tesla founder Elon Musk railed against the paper via Twitter for all sorts of offenses, from not charging the car properly, to fabricating the story entirely. Musk was indignant in the face of criticism, and while he had plenty of supporters, he had a fair number of detractors as well. He made the whole kerfuffle about him when it should have been about his product and the *New York Times*. At any other automaker, this would never have happened. Their PR team would have stepped in, kept the CEO and any other connected party on a short leash, and dealt with the problem. But Musk, who insists on being the very public face of Tesla, allowed himself to get in the middle of it. His PR team failed him by not intervening, and he gave us all a textbook example of how not to deal with a PR problem.

Indeed, this is probably the one reason why most companies or celebrities avoid getting a PR person. They honestly believe they don't do anything wrong and that they will never do anything wrong. This isn't to say that all people are beyond flawed and they should be treated as idiots, but it is a little naïve to think that you're never going to do something that harms your reputation.

We all do it. It's just that not all of us are in the public eye. You need to delicately tell a client that while they might always have the best of intentions, they might still do things that don't make a lot of sense to the audience. The client may not technically have done anything bad to cause a PR problem, but if the actions they take are *PERCEIVED* to be wrong by the audience, then that means trouble. As a PR person, you're going to have to be vigilant to prevent these issues from happening to begin with. You're going to have to keep your finger on the pulse of the world to gauge what's appropriate and what isn't in the eyes of your audience. If you're any good at your job, most of it won't be cleaning up other people's messes; it will be preventing them from ever happening in the first place.

What Is(n't) Your Client Telling You

The story of Passover is a simple one. It's one of freedom from slavery, the search for the promised land, and becoming the ancestors of the

Jewish people. Within the story itself is a parable about a father and his four sons. The father is tasked with retelling the Exodus from Egypt to his sons: one is wise, one is wicked, one is stupid, and one does not know how to even ask a question. Your client, in most cases, is the son who does not know how to ask a question, and you are the father, trying to explain that having a slice of toast is going to piss off the Big Man Upstairs.

Even if you do understand what a client requires, that doesn't mean they do. Many clients don't even know which end is up, which is part of the reason they came to you in the first place. Still, chances are they will resist your suggestions, if only because they think you are trying to get more money out of them for your "services." But stand firm. In the client-PR relationship, you are the professional and you are the one who is supposed to have all the answers. It's better that the client disagrees with your strategy than acts apathetic or clueless.

When the client doesn't know what they want, it can be very tough on your relationship. Lots of stops and starts, constant mixed signals and miscommunication. One of the best ways to avoid that is to have a prospective client answer a list of questions for you before you begin to work together. Imagine if you could do that with potential dates. Wouldn't that make life easier? That's why eHarmony works so well, provided everyone's honest.

Here is my basic questionnaire checklist for assessing the needs of a potential new client:

▶ Why do you need PR services?

▶ What PR tools have you used in the past?

▶ How is your reputation working for you?

▶ How is your reputation not working for you?

▶ Where do you want to be seen or written about?

▶ What are your current PR needs?

▶ What do you want to see as a result of PR?

▶ What marketing tools do you already use?

▶ How is the company seen in your market?

▶ What will make you happy with our relationship?

▶ What are your goals?

▶ What is your current PR strategy?

▶ What have you already done to promote yourself?

▶ What other PR people have you worked with?

▶ How did that work well for you?

▶ What didn't work well for you?

▶ Who is your audience?

▶ Who is your target audience?

▶ Do you have a brand?

▶ How would you characterize your brand?

▶ What do you feel you bring to your market?

▶ How do you feel you can improve your services?

▶ What services do you offer?

▶ What do you do that no one else can do?

▶ What is your story?

▶ How have you succeeded?

▶ What mistakes have been made?

▶ Do you think you are connecting with your audience?

That questionnaire checklist may seem extensive or even excessive, but it's intentional. You want to get a clear idea of what a client might be expecting from you, with as little room for ambiguity as possible. Of course, there are some clients who might not be able to answer those questions. They may even have no idea what you're talking about. Don't be surprised if those are the bulk of your clients when starting out. You're likely to get people who have no clue what they want. That's why you're there. Take the initiative and use your superb intellect and common sense to extract the answers from them and guide them towards an appropriate PR strategy. How you'll execute that is up to you.

Prep for the Client Meeting

If you use my questionnaire checklist, you will have a long form that includes a lot of answers to your questions, but you will still need to meet with the client. Communication is largely nonverbal, and emailing back and forth will not suffice when you're dealing with something this sensitive. An in-person meeting is usually best, since they can't hang up on you when you start to poke and prod a little, but Skype or conference call will suffice if a face-to-face meeting is not in the cards—beggars can't be choosers. Still, push for that in-person meeting because you'll get a much better handle on what they're all about by actually making their acquaintance. Plus, they might let something slip that ends up being very revealing, whether through their words or their body language. So pay attention.

Do your own research on the client and their reputation. What are the consumer reviews and forum users saying about them? What kind of press have they gotten recently? Are they using social media to interact with their customers? Use this information to assemble a dossier for your client. They may not be overly enthusiastic about what you've discovered, but there's no use in living in the fantasyland of "ought to be." You are dealing with reality, and it's important they know that as well. This also lets you compare how the client perceives themselves with how they are viewed by the public. The two can be vastly different, and when this happens, your expertise is of greatest value and most urgent need.

The information you glean, whether good or bad, is your guidebook to correcting and/or managing the client's reputation. In addition, the client may get an eye-opening look at how the message they want to disseminate isn't getting out the way they want. You may have ideas about forging your own path or being innovative, and the client may not want to emulate the competition, but successful methods are successful for a reason. At this stage, you should be adopting these methods and tweaking them slightly for your own use.

Once you've established how things really are, then you can start talking about what direction the client wants to go. Don't be surprised if the client can't articulate this. Think about how many people talk about wanting to get rich or lose weight or climb Mount Everest. Not many of them have clear, articulated goals about how they're going to achieve this, do they? And the ones who do have them tend to succeed. It's the difference between desire and ambition. Your long-term goal as a PR person is to have as many clients in the latter pile as possible.

When discussing PR strategy with your clients, don't be afraid to poke or prod (within reason). Get them to think big, to talk about their hopes and dreams. That's why they got into their business in the first place. If you are adept at steering the conversation, they'll start to talk about the ways they want to grow, as well as their frustrations with current progress.

Even though the fledgling PR professional inside of you might be worried that asking too many questions may seem like you're not qualified for the job, let that idea go. How else will you figure out what your client wants? Your boss might also think you're asking too many questions. If that's the case, ignore him. There is simply no better way to make informed decisions about what's best for your client.

Make a Plan

At some point, the client will want to see what your plans are for their PR strategy. Don't panic. The reason you asked all those questions was to elicit as much information as possible so you could draw up an accurate, detailed plan to help them.

Don't just focus on how you'll help them make their reputation better. Give them tangible examples of how you will respond to crises and what follow-up steps might be necessary in order to ensure the client's reputation stays intact. Sometimes, this isn't even about creating a plan—it's about finding out what they might do and stopping it in advance.

A great deal of firms will create a theoretical "crisis plan"— usually made up of who will be the contact point, how the agency will respond (in a logistical sense), and roughly what to do. The problem with this is there're rarely assumed worst-case scenarios. For example, you (meaning you and your team) should go through the product and *imagine* what situations might come about.

Hypothetical client's app texts each and every person on someone's phone when they open the app. That is a potential crisis waiting to happen. You want to either A) tell the client to nix it, or

B) create a contingency plan of how to respond to the situation. In this case, you'd probably want to get the client to remove it if it ever became public.

For example, Path used to be a middling, private social network. Their brand meant little—just another social network that you could only share with up to fifty people. They then focused on creating one of the most beautiful and usable apps in the world. This took the world (and the press) by storm, rebranding Path as a *private social network* that had more meaningful and personal experiences.

However, business soon trumped brand. Stories begun to surface of Path failing to encrypt your contacts. Path's brand took that hit when David Morin, the CEO, publicly announced what he'd do to fix it. This made people feel warm, fuzzy, and well kept.

A while later, they announced that they'd hit 10 million users. It then came to light that they might have done so (according to *Valleywag,* a silicon valley tabloid) by spamming *every person on a user's contact list without permission.* Suddenly the brand had a big fat turd on top of it—sure, it was a beautiful social network, but it was more dedicated to making the owners money and getting more users than actually benefitting them.

Everybody and their mother is enthralled with this idea of "brand"—thank you, Mad Men—that you will end up using it. In fact, if you start using terms like "message" and "reputation," they'll probably look at you funny and assume you don't know what you're talking about. Better to use "brand" in the company of those heathens. In the circle of trust right here, we can use all three interchangeably while understanding the subtle differences that go along with each term.

Hypothetical client says something very rude to someone in public: Talk to the client and find out any radical opinions they have. Do they have a slightly off-kilter sense of humor? Imagine a situation where they might have said something, say, racist on Twitter. The answer is to apologize, directly and without dancing around or trying to justify the remark as anything other than a lapse of judgment.

For a real-world example, take Paula Deen's recent fall from grace. Deen and her brother Earl "Bubba" Hiers were sued for alleged sexual and racial discrimination. In her deposition, Deen admitted that she has used the N-word to describe African Americans. Once, she used it to describe a robber who put a gun to her head. Once, she claims to have used it (in a so-called "nonmean" way) to recount a conversation "between blacks."

Those last two words were from her deposition.

Fatally, she also discussed a "Southern-themed wedding" mimicking black slavery. The complaint reads that Dean once said:

"Well what I would really like is a bunch of little n—rs to wear long-sleeve white shirts, black shorts, and black bow-ties, you know in the Shirley Temple days, they used to tap dance around."

She allegedly also said that it would be "a true Southern wedding, wouldn't it? But we can't do that because the media would be on me about that."

My final quote:

"Most—most jokes are about Jewish people, rednecks, black folks. Most jokes target—I don't know. I didn't make up the jokes, I don't know," said Deen. "They usually target, though, a group. Gays or straights, black, redneck, you know, I just don't know—I just don't know what to say. I can't, myself, determine what offends another person."

First and foremost, whoever media trained or does Deen's PR should be fired. Out of a cannon. Into the sun. While I can't speak for her lawyer's preparation, somebody should have prepared for the (huge) chance that she might be asked about racism. And rehearsed her not to do this.

The testimony itself was taken **May 17, 2013.** It was reported **June 19, 2013.**

A theoretical PR firm could have met with Deen anywhere between **May 1 and May 16** to discuss what she should say. Perhaps they could have discussed, bluntly, what she was going to say on the various issues. Perhaps they could have told her "if they ask if you make racist or anti-Semitic jokes, say you don't agree with them. If you've used them in the past, show regret and say it was bad judgment."

Deen went on to release three cuts of a forty-six-second video. The first was edited in a weird, disjointed fashion—the second and third less-so. The wording was awkward. The apologies less-than convincing.

In short, nobody thought to prepare her for this eventuality. They should have:

▶ Listened to the deposition as it happened.

▶ Prepared a plan based on that and imagined the worst possible situation.

   ▪ The worst possible situation actually happened: the *National Enquirer,* a national tabloid known for celebrity gossip, broke the story.

▶ Prepared the videos and made sure Paula was **not** sounding like a bizarre marketing machine going to work.

▶ Made sure Paula went to every single interview. Paula skipped her first with the Today Show. Though she went back for a second, it was still a bad situation for everybody involved.

Paula ended up losing several huge endorsement deals and her contract with the Food Network.

You want to show that you're not just thinking about the day-to-day stuff, but about possible problems. Articulating a long-term vision doesn't hurt either, but you'll have to talk to them about where they see themselves down the road for that to be anything but you spinning your wheels.

Don't be discouraged if you submit a plan and the client rejects it. That just eliminated a whole plethora of possibilities you no longer have to worry about, so you can narrow your focus. It's an opportunity to ask them more, pointed questions and refine the plan further. Here's a dirty little trade secret: most plans are never followed. They are either rejected outright or deviated from in the heat of the moment. Still, you need to show that you are proactive and organized, and that is what a plan does for you.

The first thing to do is figure out your client's brand (if it even exists) and if it needs an overhaul. You've probably heard the term a million times before—"brand"—and you may not have any idea what it means. Most people don't, if you want to know the truth. "Brand" is really just a fancy buzzword for the message your client is trying to get out combined with the reputation they have developed in the process. The balance of those two elements—message and reputation—goes a long way in determining how successful your client has been in controlling their pitch and just how much they need you.

An example of an awesome brand is Hipmunk, a website and app for finding and booking hotels and flights. They have a cute little chipmunk as their mascot, their product has always focused on being quick and easy to use, and they've always been quick to answer questions on Twitter. Alexis Ohanian (college roommate of Reddit founder Steve Huffman) worked as their advisor to help position themselves as the no-bullshit travel brand. And they succeeded. Hipmunk has been featured just about anywhere a travel brand can be and has hundreds of thousands of users. They knew what they were doing from the very beginning and executed on that vision. Any additions they made to the product were in line with said vision. Or brand, I should say.

An example of a tumultuous brand is Dell. Once regarded as the bastion of all home PC shopping, Dell fell from grace as it became common knowledge that their laptops would crap out on you, and their customer services were manned by script-reading outsourced agents. They spent years in the doldrums as customers flocked to a PC industry that was quickly catching up on price and beating them soundly at build quality, along with Apple's more affordable iMac and Mac Mini lines. Eventually, Dell began to produce PCs and laptops that were worth a damn, including the Dell XPS One 27", one of the best-available all-in-one PCs on the market.

Now, in 2013, CEO Michael Dell is pitching the board to take the company private. Their social media staff is run from America, and their customer care has somewhat improved. Their computers are competitively priced and relatively reliable.

And yet the cost cutting of outsourcing and poor customer care has bruised the brand significantly.

With the advent of social media taking everyone public, everybody and their mother is so enthralled with this idea of "brand"—thank you, Mad Men—that you will end up using it. In fact, if you start using terms like "message" and "reputation," they'll probably look at you funny and assume you don't know what you're talking about. Better to use "brand" in the company of those heathens. In the circle of trust right here, we can use all three interchangeably while understanding the subtle differences that go along with each term.

Case Study: The North Face

For an example of how branding really works, and how it ties into message and reputation, let's look at The North Face.

By keeping its designs contemporary and its prices high, The North Face has expanded beyond its early adventurous demographic to become a premium clothing brand. You have to have a lot of disposable income to afford their gear, and the very nature of high-end outerwear suggests that you partake in high-brow activities like heli-skiing or hanging out in the lodge at some exclusive winter resort in some far-off exotic land.

Of course, there's another important element to The North Face brand that is very prominent, though not officially touted in their actual message: their jackets are extremely popular with a lot of rap artists and have been a fixture in hip-hop culture for years. Rappers have bragged about wearing (and stealing) their jackets in rap lyrics, and they've worn their stuff in music videos as symbols of affluence and style rather than as paid spokespeople. Hip-hop fans recognize and appreciate the connection between the music and the product. While this is counter to the audience The North Face is supposedly targeting, it has become a well-understood aspect of their reputation and a sizeable contribution to the company's bottom line. The urban, hip-hop crowd may not be the brand's intended target but they are still part of its audience all the same.

Brands that find themselves in a similar situation have a decision to make with respect to the message they want to send and the reputation they have developed. Do you give into the latter and abandon the former? Do you double down on the former and push away the latter? Or do you find the balance, servicing both in as copasetic a way as possible? That is the route The North Face took, to great success. Cristal, the famous champagne maker popular with the hip-hop crowd, went the other way and tried to hang on too tightly to their snooty, high-brow self-image only to find themselves in the middle of a boycott led by Jay-Z in 2006.

Brand Building

If your client has a strong brand, consider yourself lucky. Not only do you have something to work with, but you can operate on numerous levels too. With The North Face, you have all kinds of different messages and audiences to play with, on both an overt and a subliminal level.

Early in your career, most of your clients will not have a brand at all. If that's the case, you'll have to help them create one before you can start pitching. A brand like The North Face has had lots of time to not only create their message, but also let other things—like rap music—shape and expand their brand identity. You don't have that luxury.

One thing you can do is put out feelers to your target audience and see what they think. While you may not like what you hear, you will also get an objective opinion on things, which will show you where to best focus your efforts.

If I get a potential product, I'll take it to two people:

▶ A tech reporter. They'll know how it'll fit into the industry, how it might play with their boss (or the rest of the media), and how they themselves might use it.

▶ My wife. She's not a huge technologist, but knows how to use a laptop and an iPhone. From her I can derive how a real person, rather than someone deeply ingrained in Silicon Valley, will accept something.

If your client has had a brand in the past, then you may want to build on that, especially if you are tasked with reviving a defunct company or brand that has some kind of "heritage" to it.

You also want the brand to be memorable and easy to relate to. If a client, PR person, or customer has to spend an hour explaining the business to someone, it's doomed. What you want to do is create a living, breathing brand with a simple story at its core and a constantly changing set of products or services that are worth keeping an eye on. Your brand idea might not catch on right away, but if you build it right it will eventually get out there.

How You'll Save a Client in a Crisis

It is a truism that everyone makes mistakes. What is even truer these days is that everyone loves to point out others' mistakes. Especially online. No matter what client you have, no matter how strong their brand, something will happen to their reputation. There will be a mistake. No matter how long you're in the PR business, you will deal with industry veterans who continue to be surprised when they get bad press, long past the point where they should be used to it. Your job as the PR person is to empathize with your client's concerns, assure them they will get through it, then get to work minimizing the damage the mistake(s) might have on their reputation. Most of your work will be online.

As a new entrant into the world of PR, I'm sure by now you've heard that old saying, "Any press is good press." Newsflash: it's not true. Not anymore, anyway. There are very few people for whom this is true. And it is never true all the time. In the Internet era, where things stay online forever and rumors can snowball into the most absurd falsehoods, bad press can be a disaster. Online readers don't check publication dates, for instance, so any bad coverage they find from months or years ago is just as likely to stick to the client today as it did when it originally happened. The trick is to know everything and deal with it like an adult instead of a scared child.

If you're diligent about doing media monitoring, then you'll find out about the bad things pretty quickly. When a wave of bad press hits, it's up to you to assess the urgency of the situation and get a clear picture of your options.

Before you respond, you should meet with the client and find out what they want to do. It's entirely possible that they may not have the same reaction you do, and their strategy may differ. As always, defend your own ideas, but defer to their opinion. They are paying you, after all.

It doesn't hurt to seek out the opinion of a third party in times like these, if only to give you more information and a different perspective. You can ask a friend, a colleague, or, even better, a PR contact that you have cultivated a relationship with via networking. They will help ground your thinking and make sure you don't do anything too crazy.

Do You Need to Respond?

The truth is you might not need to respond to certain kinds of negative online mentions. It might be one little comment in a sea of good comments. Your client might be collateral damage in an online flame war about something else. This is the dangerous part of monitoring everything being said about your client: misinterpreting or overestimating commentary online. As the primary defender of your client's reputation, your instinct is probably to respond but sometimes responding is the last thing you want to do. It might just draw more attention to the comments or stir up more dissent that then becomes a firestorm of problems for you and for your client. Remember, the quickest way to put out a fire is to starve it of oxygen.

If everybody seems happy with a product but one or two people are needlessly picking at some elements, don't wade in unless it's an easy fix. If a commenter is hating the fact that a game has a particular popup or makes a particular sound, it may be easy to remove it. However, consider that somebody else might really like it. If it's an utterly tiny point, don't touch it. And never, ever argue with them in public.

However, quick fixes can actually work to your advantage. I had a client that shared photos between friends. A reporter at *TIME* said that he hated that when he emailed his wife photos from the app it asked her to sign up, but you could easily skip said notification by hitting the escape key. The client removed the prompt and allowed anyone to view the photos without having to hit the escape. A week later, the reporter ran it as one of the top 50 Android apps of the year.

Conversely, going into comments and saying that people are wrong, or that they don't "get it," will always make you look like an over-sensitive doofus. Helpfully answering people's queries and making their lives easier is great. Arguing with them about the benefits or errors in your product makes you look infantile and over-sensitive.

Overall, while your client might be nervous about watching and waiting, there is a good reason for waiting to see what happens. Even just waiting a few hours can help you determine if this is something that even merits your attention. If the discussion doesn't seem to be moving too far away from the starting point, if it's not getting linked or forwarded around, then you may want to leave it alone and let it blow over.

If you notice that the snarky remarks are getting out of hand, however, then you do need to respond. It might mean there are more negative waves to handle, or that your client has a much deeper problem than either of you expected. Not saying anything—especially if the commentary is related to dissatisfaction and is being echoed by

EVERYONE—can be viewed negatively, particularly as weakness or indifference.

Then you've just made more problems for yourself. So if you have to respond, the next question is obviously what to say.

How Should You Respond?

In the past, being the know-it-all was the way to go. You would directly address the issues and then show that the person saying bad things is wrong and stupid. Alas, times have changed.

A new approach that seems to be working better for PR crises is to ask questions of the person saying unfavorable things about your client. See if you can get to the bottom of the real issue before you start calling them out directly for being an idiot. Asking questions, challenging their assumptions, cutting through the rhetoric and ad hominem attacks are all much more subtle, nonthreatening ways of calling out whoever is giving your client a PR headache.

Say your client's product didn't work on delivery for *one* blogger. The wrong call here would be to assume that they'll simply whine and seem irrelevant. In fact, the best call here is to be up front—say, "Hey, what's going on? That doesn't happen most of the time. How can we help?" Be as nice as possible. Try to reach out in private and smooth the situation over by offering as much technical support as possible, connecting them with the CEO, and generally getting them as much help as possible. If they're not responsive, respond in the comments—again, nicely. Even if they're unresponsive in email, don't share that with the rest of the world unless they claim you didn't email them. And if that happens, take a screenshot.

All in all, be as upfront and helpful as you can.

Now, if your client did something that was outright ludicrous, you may need to do more than just see if you can smooth things over.

When GoDaddy's CEO Bob Parsons uploaded a video in which he proudly shot and killed elephants, a flood of bad press engulfed the web host. He attempted to explain the situation as helping keep the elephant population in Zimbabwe down to stop them trampling crops and villagers. His explanation was far from satisfying. Parsons also attempted to explain his giant smile in a picture featuring him with a dead elephant:

"When you see me smiling in that picture, I'm smiling because I'm relieved no one was hurt, that the crop was saved, and that these people were going to be fed—the type of smile when you get a good report card or achieve a goal."

This was a situation that could have been avoided only if somebody had told Parsons to shut up about his elephant killing. Otherwise it's a complete nightmare for anyone new to PR, and one you shouldn't have to handle.

Of course, we are talking about big time screwups that could have serious ramifications for someone's personal reputation, their livelihood, or both. In this case, issuing a press release, calling a press conference, or issuing a carefully worded apology will be the way to go. If that's the case, you don't have too much to worry about because these moves are above your entry-level pay grade. Just pay attention and learn for when you have to handle these types of crises yourself.

That's not to say there isn't a hard-and-fast rule about responding; whatever you say should be respectful, clear, and effective.

The key is honesty. Did your client release a buggy piece of software? Then tell everyone that's what they did. Did they make a mistake in an interview? Say that. The client may think it's the end of the world, but it really isn't. Unless they are someone like BP that jeopardized the health and safety of the planet and all the creatures residing there, it will end up as a blip on life's radar.

But keep in mind, not everything in life can be salvaged, and this extends to reputation as well. As a PR person, you are duty bound to do everything you can to help boost your client's reputation, but ultimately, it is out of your hands. Their audience determines if all of your hard work will pay off. They might not be able or willing to forgive and forget. They may not want to give your client another chance.

If a client's reputation can't be healed with your efforts, it doesn't mean their reputation is completely unsalvageable. It might just be a matter of time and patience. They may just have to service those few loyal people who stuck around and then wait it out until the rest come back. When things finally die down, a large rebranding effort can take place and your client might return to their original position within their industry, or even eclipse it.

While most clients are going to want to deny, deny, deny and get their audience to come back as soon as possible, they might want to listen to your advice. It's not always about responding or taking action or even issuing an apology. Sometimes, you do just want to wait things out, especially if it all began with one person's reaction or a misstatement or a rare mistake. Stepping back may be all that is necessary. This can also give the audience a chance to take a breath and let tempers cool off.

Personally, I don't think everyone can be saved from PR night mares, but I don't ever tell clients that. I will continue to fight for them if they think the fight is worth it. And I will continue to help them smooth things over if I think they might be able to make it through. But I don't ever forget that it's not up to me in the end.

The audience is going to determine whether the client can be saved. They are going to look at the evidence, evaluate the actions, and then make their decision. Depending on the extent of the offense, the audience may never be able to forget.

You can't really tell if this will be the case, no matter how well you know the audience, but it's something to keep in mind.

Think about all of the people who treated Britney Spears with utter disgust when she shaved her head and began attacking cars in 2007. In January 2008 she was hospitalized after seemingly being under the influence of an unknown substances at her home. She was later put under a 5150 involuntary psychiatric hold and temporary conservatorship of her father. Five days later, she was released. By September 2008 she was hosting the MTV Video Music Awards, and by December she had released her sixth studio album *Circus*. In March 2009 she took it on tour. Just over a year later and the world had forgotten her missteps.

Fast forward to 2012 and she's released several albums and made $15 million as one of the judges of the music competition show *The X Factor*.

Not only did she recover, she came back stronger than ever.

Of course, there will inevitably come a time when you need to tell a client that you've done all you can. You can show them what you have done, and you can try to explain to them that this is your best effort.

You might feel it's your responsibility to stick it out with them, but as soon as you've exhausted your resources, you need to move away. You have other clients to help and other reputations to support. You have to let them know that you have done what you can, but you're out of ideas, and they may want to find another PR agency.

Just as you can't guarantee that something will go viral, you also can't guarantee that someone's reputation will stay intact forever. That's not to say that PR is a shot in the dark. By working on your pitches, writing them clearly and carefully, targeting your audience, learning about the industry and building a strong brand, you are taking proactive steps to ensure your client's success.

And it still may not work. It's okay. It's not any fault of yours and it doesn't mean that you're not a good PR person. Some clients just aren't going to be someone YOU can represent. There are other people who can step in and help this one. Live to fight another day.

You can't guarantee results. You can guarantee hard work and dedication to their cause and to their reputation, but not results. From there, it's all up to the audience, to the media, and to whatever intangible force you think is in charge of someone's reputation. As long as you give the client a realistic understanding of your ability and make the best effort possible, you can be satisfied that you did everything you could for the client.

pitching

case study ··

Three or four months after my baptism-by-fire in the PR world, I had my first taste of success. My then-boss had cajoled a strange yet likeable British man into giving the firm some money, and for that, we were retained to launch an e-reader at a time when they were still very, very expensive. This e-reader was slightly cheaper than the Kindle (one of only a few on the market), which made it remarkable. Nowadays, you can open a cereal box and find an e-reader as a prize. It was my job to promote it, and all I could see was that it was being horribly over-blown in terms of coverage. All anyone would care about was that it came in a few different colors, it held a lot of books, and it was cheaper than the Kindle. Yes, there was some bollocks in there about book formatting and refresh rate, and the e-book industry or whatever, but it came down to those few very simple points:

- It was cheaper than the Kindle.
- It was coming out very soon.
- Journalists could actually touch it.
- It came in multiple colors.

Everyone tutted about not knowing what to do with it, so I just started sending out three-sentence emails about what it was, when it was ready, and whether the reporter wanted to meet up with the CEO of the e-reader company to see it and ask some questions. People (including me) were stunned at the response—top-line reporters from the *New York Times, Wall Street Journal, WIRED,* and other outlets agreed to meetings. I was hailed as the firm's Pied Piper of Reporters, able to secure nineteen meetings in only a few days. I sat there and basked in the adulation, bathing in my own pathetic ego-musk, when all I really did was talk like a normal person and mention the things that I'd give a shit about if I were the one reading an email. I tried to tell my bosses that I wasn't doing anything magical, and they continued to ignore it, insisting that I was "hiding something."

Other clients, including a genetics social network that I somehow got on TechCrunch and USAToday, were a roaring success. Again, I worked my "magic," which meant that I'd read a publication, wrote down a few things that I knew the reporter would like, and pitched them the same old story with a different intro. I should also say that my emails still sucked—they were still 350 words, still bulky and unwieldy, but I tried to keep it as human and normal as possible.

Eventually I left that firm and joined the last firm I would ever work for before going out on my own. Over the next two and a half years I made a point of getting to know as many people as possible on a personal level. I'd reach out to them to say hello, use "not a pitch" in the subject line of my emails, and tell them that the next time they were in New York, drinks were on me. The General Manager of the firm had given me a business AMEX to help facilitate. I didn't go crazy, but I managed to build up quite the contact list simply by not talking about work until reporters brought it up themselves. People thought I was some sort of PR savant. All I was doing was treating people well and caring about them beyond the "what can you do for me?" transactional level. My approach worked. It turns out that "not a pitch" is still being used among people in the industry as an email subject line.

The Reader Determines the Pitch

If there was a formula for success in the PR world, I would have been able to avoid my own version of PR boot camp upon starting out and I wouldn't be here writing this book to help you get through it. Instead, I'd be selling the formula to every single PR neophyte and swimming in my Scrooge McDuck money-pool.

While there is no formula, there is one skill you can learn that will dramatically increase your chances of succeeding in PR. That skill is pitching. More than networking or power lunches or crisis management, pitching is the bedrock of PR. Not everybody is good at it. But if you are, your career trajectory will be limitless.

The goal of pitching is to get in and get out as quickly as possible with the result that you want. There is no fluff. You are not here to communicate everything all at once either. You are here to get them to do something, in an honest and up-front way. Pitching can then expand to everything else—a press release, a forum post, a tweet, a Facebook post.

Before you begin to write anything, you need to think about one thing: the reader. The reader might be your client, their fans, another reporter, and sometimes even the competition or a rival PR firm. All that matters is what the reader wants to hear and what they need to know. If you don't keep your reader in mind, you're not going to write anything that gets read or that gets noticed. Your reader might not give a shit about your client. They might even hate them. They could love them too, sure, but most of the time in PR you're pitching a reporter who has no idea who your client is.

Close your eyes and put yourself in the shoes of a typical reporter in today's newsroom: underpaid, overworked, always under the gun to "produce content" like some kind of animal whose sole purpose is to breed. They're in the middle of their day. They have 250 other emails in their inbox. You have probably thirty seconds of their time. They may or may not like your client.

They will determine whether your pitch is ultimately successful or not, so write with those limitations in mind.

Before You Pitch: Do Your Homework

A large part of what will make your pitch successful has nothing to do with how well you express yourself. The battle is won or lost before you even sit down to pitch. What do I mean by that? Well, you need to do your homework. This is a multifaceted approach to keeping your eyes and ears open. You need to not only be supremely knowledgeable about the industry you are covering, but also the big players, journalists, and even the other PR firms in your space.

The easiest way to do this is to read constantly. Keep up with every single newspaper article, trade publication, magazine, and blog that is relevant (not just out there for your consumption). And by "relevant" I mean a trusted source of good information. There's plenty of crap out there, so ask people for recommendations. They'll help you figure out what to read, what to read first, and what not to read at all.

The immediate payoff here for someone new to the business is that you'll sound like you know which end is up. You're constantly learning and your opinions will change fluidly as new information comes to light, but having a baseline understanding of your industry goes a long way. I can converse on the same level as most veteran reporters and that makes me someone they look forward to speaking with. I'm not there to pander or waste their time or spout off a lot of bullshit. Instead, we can have a conversation as equals and relate to one another on a mutually interesting level. Nobody cares where I went to school, or that I like running, or that I drink lots of coffee. They care that I can speak confidently on the issues that matter to their job, their industry, and, if you're lucky enough to work for clients with global reach, the world.

There's a fun side to this as well. Since I cover tech stuff, my "homework" often involves a lot of hands-on time with new products. That means I get to play with every new gadget under the sun—strictly for "professional" reasons, of course. None of that playtime would be of much use though if I didn't also know things like how Android and iOS work, or how the app store ecosystems for both differ. See? Along with the fun stuff comes the hard work.

The Story

A story is what you'll actually be pitching to journalists when you want them to write about your client. It's the pitch you're pitching. Confused? Don't be. Think of it like this: Pitching is how you get reporters to write about your client. The pitch is the story you want them to write. I talked about it in the first chapter if you want to refresh your memory. I'll wait.

Like novels or screenplays, there are generally a few simple story frameworks that everybody uses when building the pitch that they're going to pitch to reporters. There can be crossover among the genres, but they don't usually deviate from the basic structure. Here are the four that you'll need to know when you start out in PR.

Company Story

"X Company Is the Y for Z"—this happens a great deal in technology, be it for a new website or a new product. Socialcam (a video-recording social network acquired for $42m) was the "Instagram for video," Instagram was the "Facebook for pictures." These analogs and schemata are the way people relate to the world.

Asking someone, "Will you write about this?" is the surest path to outright rejection. You have to frame your request with a good reason (preferably more than one) for the writer to report on it. Do your homework and find out whether the outlet does straight-up profiles of companies or if they require an "angle." The tech media is always hungry for good stories on new or interesting companies, but they also get pitched on them multiple times a day, so make sure you do everything you can to pique their interest. You may be able to get away with a story on the company itself, or your pitch may need to incorporate a unique angle like how the founder's inspiration came from getting left at the altar.

Company News

"X Company Launches Y"—a company may receive $2m in funding for their new venture. Or they may hire a new CEO. This is actually a good way to get a company story—you need some news to tie into. Many industries, especially technology, treat funding announcements as big events. "Funding," in this case, refers to when a company receives money from investors in return for a part of the company.

For example, that company who received $2m in funding may have accepted it in exchange for 10% of the company. This means the full value of the company is $20m (if 10% is worth $2m, then 100% is $20m). That can be a big story for financial outlets, whose readers can earn or lose money in their various investment positions based on this information.

Trend Pieces

These are a little more difficult to pitch. You'll need a "big picture" view that helps tie your client into a larger theme. Say your client has created an app that can help gardeners. Your pitch could be tied into the growing (no pun intended) trend in urban vertical gardening. There's also a food element in this story, which is another hot trend these days, especially local, organic, and sustainable produce, like the kind grown by your client's target audience. You can even combine them and hint at a new trend that few people are aware of called "foodscaping." In this instance, you're pitching your client as both on trend *and* ahead of the curve. That's the best place to be.

Sourcing

Are you working with a privacy lawyer? They may be an excellent talking head or someone who can provide a quote to a reporter. Many CEOs or members of a company are able to speak on subjects, but they often need someone who can put them in touch with the right media figures.

Sit down and read a story in the paper, and you'll inevitably see someone quoted—a lawyer, a doctor, a person of interest within the story who isn't necessarily part of it. For example, I introduced a reporter to a client that makes Android apps more user friendly when they were working on a story about the user interfaces of new phones. Unsurprisingly, the reporter was happy, because the client was actually useful to them. The client was happy because they got their name associated with a big story.

Just make sure they're intelligent and saying something new, not about the company. You are effectively playing matchmaker for a reporter in this situation. Just make sure your client knows that they should provide a direct answer to the reporter's questions, not use it as an opportunity to plug their business or themselves.

The Game Is Won or Lost Before It Even Begins

Basketball fans will remember NBA legend Allen Iverson for more than just his play. Iverson was the subject of an epic meltdown at a press conference about skipping out on practice. Iverson's response was indignant. "We're sitting here, I'm supposed to be the franchise player, and we're in here talking about practice?" he asked. Small wonder that Iverson left the NBA disgraced and is now broke, while Kobe Bryant, a player known for his obsessive conditioning routines, is still one of the best in the league.

You can become the Kobe Bryant of PR, but only if you practice *and* play like Kobe. You don't need to hit the weight room or the treadmill like he does—though, trust me, it's a great way to blow off steam—you just need to hit the PR version of those things.

An Iverson-like approach to PR would be to breeze in every day, nose in the air, and rely on your natural charm or writing skill to send the same damn pitch to all sorts of reporters, without putting any thought into who they are. You will have some success because you are capable of making your client sound appealing, but not nearly as much as you would if you took a Kobe-style approach. Ultimately, you do yourself a disservice with the Iverson approach. Remember that every person you are contacting is a human being, not a means to an end. You must give a shit about them, and sending out the same boilerplate pitch (or even a slightly tweaked one) is a great way to show that you think of them only as a way to get coverage for your client, a cog in the wheel.

I know that in many situations, your boss will tell you to start pitching people right away and it will be difficult to do things the way I outline below. They do this because they don't know any better. It's okay. There will be plenty of other opportunities down the road to do things properly. And if you learn them now, you'll be prepared for those opportunities when they come.

The right way to do things is a meticulous, personalized process that requires the kind of time and investment a world-class athlete like Kobe Bryant puts into his own practice. You not only know the client's most intimate details, but the bloggers, journalists, and writers on an equally detailed level. You don't even have to know them personally to start. Simple things like Google searches will yield huge results. Look at the tone of their writing, how they articulate themselves, and other textual cues. Are they casual, formal, fond of flowery prose? Do they love to talk about themselves (or maybe somebody important to them)? Do they mention hobbies or outside interests? You need to play a bit of the detective here, assembling a dossier on your person of interest. Social media profiles are an even more intimate glimpse into what these people are all about. Peruse them at length.

Feel free to start interacting with them on social media. Don't try and impress them with how smart or cool you are. Just be yourself. In fact, if you don't know anything, asking a question is an amazing way to show that you not only exist, but that you're interested in them and their field. Do this with a number of reporters and let them get to know who you are. When it comes time to pitch them, doing so will feel natural, like a conversation between acquaintances. Not like somebody obliging them with an annoying favor.

The Nuts and Bolts

Imagining the reporter as a smart teenager is a good way to measure how plainly written your pitch is. You don't want to condescend to them by any means, but using the same kind of language an undergraduate sociology professor uses is the wrong approach as well. As with most important things in life, practice is the best way to get better. Your objective is to deliver the most information with the least amount of words. It is not an opportunity for you to make yourself sound smart or hip, but a chance to convey key concepts to whoever your audience is. Nothing more.

And still, ninety-five percent of pitches go right into the garbage. Why? Because they are awful. They're awful because PR people try to shine shit or make their client into something they're not and can never be. They write pitches full of words like "leverage" or "revolutionary." They write long, long emails that make no sense and are brutal to read. Don't be that person. Give a shit about what you do, and remember that your time and your reader's time are valuable.

Personally, I have three hard rules I stick to at all costs when I am composing a pitch.

The Three Rules
•••••••••••••••••••••

1. It's under 200 words.

2. It must be direct and free of jargon or fluff.

3. It's written, not copy-pasted. Write each pitch individually, for each person, each time.

When you follow these rules, you can craft something that is valuable not just to your client, but to the reporter on the other end as well. Reporters don't need "stories" per se (which is a distinct concept from the "story" we discussed above). They have plenty to write about. What your pitch should do is not give them a "story" that helps them write something about your client, but instead shares some kind of information that is useful to them and their readers. Just as you are providing a service to your client by helping them get coverage, you are also providing a service to the reporter by giving them high-quality material to use as content for their publication.

The Headline

You're going to have to craft a good headline. Headlines are so important that newspapers used to keep a writer on staff whose only job was to write headlines. Nowadays, that job is gone thanks to massive budget cuts, but the headline's importance remains the same. Especially in an era when attention spans are shrinking and the amount of content vying for that attention is exploding. Your headline must be focused, to the point, and interesting enough to draw your audience in further.

A general rule of thumb is that your headline should reflect as much of the pitch's information as possible. If you write a headline that doesn't reflect your pitch, there's a good chance the reader will feel like you were trying to mislead them or, worse, waste their time. That's a great way to ensure your failure as a PR person.

Some find that writing the content first makes it easier to come up with a headline, while others swear that having the title first makes the writing easier. Personally, I prefer the latter. It'll hone you in on what you're really trying to say versus trying to find a five-word description of everything you've written.

The audience—in this case, a writer reading your pitch—doesn't have the time, and they're certainly not getting paid to hear you babble on. If they are a blogger or reporter (and in most cases, they will be), they're getting paid to write things. Make the most of it and respect the gift of their time by only saying what needs to be said.

After You Email

Just because you've sent the email pitch doesn't mean your work is done. Even when you do email a reporter a really specific pitch, they may not respond. Don't harass them. Give them a few days between replies—follow up once, maybe twice—then just let it go. You only want to hound them if they've shown interest in your work and they've suddenly gone dark. If they've never responded, well, that's just how it goes. You're not going to win them all.

I talked about ToutApp earlier. It's not just good for seeing who is opening your emails; it also shows you who is deleting them right away. Don't sweat it if your emails go unread or blown off at first. There will be instances where things don't go your way, and you will have to face the music. A few years ago, there was a reporter at a major magazine who was the target of what I thought was good-natured ribbing about a story he wrote. I teased him on Twitter for writing a story that I thought was awfully similar to another journalist's. The reporter took this very harshly, calling me names and warning me not to give reporters too much crap; after all, we'll need them one day.

Being the smart-ass I am, I gave it back to him better than I got it. He backed off and I figured that was the end of it. Now he works at a really major publication and won't return my emails. What's the moral of this story? Don't be a dick. If you fuck up, say you're sorry. You may lose a client, or your job. Guess what? You'll bounce back.

Clients and jobs will always come and go, but you'll be screwed if you have no media contacts, or worse, become known for being the guy who tells reporters to go fuck themselves. That's another great way to ensure failure in PR.

Pitching by Phone

Nearly everybody today has a smartphone. These are some of the most powerful computers ever created by mankind, and we use them for the most inane purposes. Imagine telling somebody from the Renaissance period that in 2013 we have handheld machines that can access the aggregate of human achievement and enable instant voice-to-voice communication, but all we use them for is to watch videos of cats while we poop.

I'd encourage you to avoid making phone calls. Emails can be annoying, but an unscheduled phone call is invasive and always a bad idea from that standpoint. There is a contingent of people, however, who don't want to be pitched over email. They just think it's another form of spam, no matter how sincere you might be. It will only happen every so often, but you'll have to be ready to engage these types over the phone when it does.

Before you dial, have a thirty- to sixty-second pitch ready to go. Do NOT script it. Get an idea of what you want to say and how you want to say it. No "umms" or "ahhs" or any filler words. By forcing them to stick to a script, you're guaranteeing that any deviation will lead to an instant hesitation.

The pitch should do three things: Let the reporter know who you are, who your client is, and what exactly is worth reporting on. It should also be easy to understand and make sense to the person you're calling. As a courtesy to the reporter, make sure you know their name and pronounce it correctly. As someone with an obscure last name, I know that having my name pronounced correctly is always a nice surprise. Ask them if they are free to talk for a minute. If not, thank them, bid them good-bye, and hang up. Don't charge ahead with your pitch and act like an inconsiderate jerk; you risk burning that bridge forever. Remember, you can always call back another time.

Though I don't think any decent reporter is going to argue with you about the substance of your pitch or the nature of your client's business when you're on the phone pitching them, it never hurts to be ready for your own on-the-spot interview.

Some of the common questions you might be asked are:

▶ Why is this better than X?

▶ <Insert difficult technical question.>

▶ Why are you calling me?

It can help to prepare your answers to these questions ahead of time. There are two ways to think about this.

One, you can answer their questions as honestly as possible.

Or two, you can answer their questions with more questions. This is generally a risk but one that you can mitigate by making sure your questions are good ones; better ones in fact. This is not a move for amateurs. If the writer is an expert in their field (common with reporters who cover specific industries, companies, or people), they will crucify you if you obfuscate or bullshit them. On the other hand, honesty always builds respect between two people. Keep the conversation light and easy, and don't spend too much time trying to convince someone who seems angry or overly critical.

Turning Around a Bad Phone Call

When you start to get that feeling that your phone call isn't going as well as you planned, you will be tempted to hang up and pretend your cell provider dropped the call. Don't. This is when you need to double down and approach the phone call like a pro.

At some point in your career you are going to start getting uncomfortable calls about your client where the person on the other end of the line tosses around accusations and screams at you. Don't worry about it or take it to heart. When it happens just know that you're finally playing in the major leagues. Right now, you're a minor leaguer at best, and the stakes are low so no reporter worth their salt is going to waste their energy on you. That's why now is the perfect time to learn how to salvage a pitch call.

First things first, keep a cool head. I know, I know, easier said than done. On an instinctual level, it's easy to react. Without even knowing it you can find yourself matching their tone of voice and their energy (i.e., yelling right back at them and losing your shit). This will not help your PR reputation. Instead, lower your voice and slow down your breathing. Take a deep breath. It's cliché, I know, but it really does work, so do it. Feel your heart rate slow down and let the color come back into your face. Are you calm and collected now? Good. Time to approach it like a professional.

Ask them why they are upset. This is a very subtle, nonthreatening way of calling out someone on their uncouth behavior. If they are a decent, rational person, they will usually back down and explain their frustration, or even apologize. If you have some finesse and even a hint of empathy in your voice, this is something you can achieve.

If the person on the other end of the phone keeps screaming at you and making a fuss, then thank them for their time and hang up. Whether they are a client or someone you are trying to pitch is irrelevant. You don't want or need those people as clients or a part of your network.

The Press Release Lie

Writing press releases will be a common part of your job. Typically used for more informative topics rather than to sell or persuade like an ad or a sales letter, a press release is a quasi-news story, written in the third person, by you, about your client in service of their goals. When done at the right time, in the right way, a press release can be helpful in a number of different event-type scenarios:

▶ Introducing a new player to an industry,

▶ Introducing a new product or service, and

▶ Announcing an organizational change.

In theory, a press release is a way of adding credibility and legitimacy to these events you're trying to publicize. Given their periodic nature, however, it shouldn't be a surprise if you don't write many press releases in a given year. It's okay. You shouldn't constantly be announcing things. In fact, you don't want to be, for a couple of reasons: 1) if everything is a big announcement, then nothing is a big announcement, and 2) in practice, press releases are pretty useless.

Over the course of your career, if you stick with it, many clients will ask you to put out many press releases because they think they're something they should have. The truth of the matter is that most news is disseminated via pitching. Press releases don't really work without pitching, in fact. These days, press releases come in most often *behind* the pitch to provide all the information you didn't initially include. They're then put out on newswires where no one reads them. One notable exception is the auto industry, where press releases are still popular. With autos, press releases are a good way to explain a lot of complex, arcane facts and figures, but this is an anomaly.

In the grand scheme of things, you will write and release dozens of press releases on behalf of clients for the same reason you listen to your mother and invite someone you don't like to your wedding. It's expected of you, therefore you do it.

Press Release Basics

Writing a press release is far easier than you might realize. There's even a template you can use, and I've included it below. Before you begin, it can help to look at the wire service's guidelines for press releases, just to make sure your press release conforms to their expectations. Check to see what they need from you and what you can expect from them.

For example, if you are writing about a new product, you'll need to include the following:

▶ What it does,

▶ What it will cost,

▶ Where it will be found for purchase,

▶ How it is better than before, and

▶ How it was created.

Think about how you might explain a piece of breaking news in conversation to a person you've never met. If your client is releasing a new album, for instance, you might want to include when it will be released, the client's background (past albums), prior album sales numbers, etc.

Here is a template I use:

FOR IMMEDIATE RELEASE

NAME (Your Name)

NUMBER (Your Number)

EMAIL (Your Email)

MAIN TITLE FOR PRESS RELEASE
Subtitle for Press Release

(LOCATION, STATE)

It should usually have a basic intro saying that the company has released whatever it has released and then explaining what that thing is. It'll maybe involve a quote or two, saying how excited they are about it, or who the partner involved is.

xxxxxxxxxxx press release content xxxxxxxxxxxxxxxx

xxxxxxxxxxx press release content xxxxxxxxxxxxxxxx

xxxxxxxxxxx press release content xxxxxxxxxxxxxxxx

xxxxxxxxxxx press release content xxxxxxxxxxxxxxxx

xxxxxxxxxxx press release content xxxxxxxxxxxxxxxx

(This can go on for a few paragraphs, but no more than one document page.)

###

Contact Information

That's all there is to it: A simple setup that allows you to express the information you hope the audience wants to hear in as clear and concise a way as possible. You may find that different press release resources have different ideas about formatting, so double check with them before you submit something with this format.

Five Rules for Press Releases

The basics and the template will give you what you need to write a real press release. These other rules will help you write a press release someone might actually read.

1. **Don't make it longer than 400 words**—longer releases are not only more expensive to put on the wire, but people's attention spans are not that long anymore. Like I said earlier, your goal is to say as much in as few words as you can.

2. **Don't try to be funny**—press releases are pieces of dry, professional writing designed to convey information. Humor obscures that at times. Plus, you're probably not as funny as you think you are.

3. **Proofread it twice**—don't ever release anything onto the wire before you've meticulously checked your spelling and grammar. Press releases make the rounds very quickly online. If the client or the error is important enough, it could be the one seen around the world that follows you or your client for a long time.

4. **Target the right media**—to make sure your pitch or press release gets read, it needs to get to the right places, where your message will be received, heard, seen, shared, and retweeted.

5. **Have something of value to share**—without it you may not get the help you want or need. Start building a message that makes sense to share with the media you have targeted. Find the right reporter and let them own the story. Make them believe that you tailored it just for them. They may still hate it, but they'll respect your efforts.

Today, the public is the media and the media is your audience. The media, specifically online news outlets, are increasingly reliant on blogs, press releases, and PR campaigns for their "content." Budgets are smaller, deadlines are tighter, and reporters are under an unprecedented amount of pressure to deliver more content—but not necessarily better journalism. This is a unique opportunity for you as a PR person. With the right approach you can play an enormous part in influencing the message that gets disseminated.

A Brief Lesson in Lead Times

It might be a slightly foreign concept to those with no media background, but each publication has a different lead time between when they conceive of a story and when it actually gets published.

Blogs tend to have shorter lead times due to the fact that they are on the Internet and have an infinite amount of space to fill with a seemingly infinite amount of competition. As a result, they tend to sacrifice accuracy in the name of speed, so you'll need to be very quick when dealing with them and make sure what you give them is as clear and correct as possible. On the right blog with the right story, one post, no matter how wildly inaccurate, can spread like wildfire and become gospel before you have a chance to fix it.

When the Boston bombing happened, many blogs and news sites were quick (one might say too quick) to report on what they heard from social media, unverified reports, and other situations. This led to a great deal of hysteria about the potential casualties and damage from the bombing. While an immensely extreme reaction, the speed at which information travels means that people can and will take something, even something incorrect, and run with it.

There are also blogs out there, run by publications like the *New York Times* and other established outlets, that operate on similar timeframes to normal blogs, but also have editorial lines of defense, including a copyeditor. This gives them the flexibility to do a story quickly if necessary, but also means a story is more likely to get fact-checked and edited.

Newspapers can operate quickly, but they are limited by physical distribution. They only publish once a day, not once an hour like some blogs. Hence, the fastest they can humanly get something written and published is twenty-four hours. This means they need to work with you a little more carefully on a story, and that they'll have to get things checked and re-checked by their editors (including a copyeditor, section editor, or editor-in-chief, depending on how large the paper is). This isn't a bad thing though. If anything, they're taking extra time to ensure that the story is correct.

Magazines, on the other hand, take their sweet-ass time, but this is because the process of publishing a magazine can take a few months from start to finish. The exceptions are weekly periodicals like *TIME* and *US Weekly*. Glossy magazines like *Maxim, Cosmopolitan,* or *Men's Health* all have a three- to four-month lead time. Pitching something that'll launch in March? Go to them in December. It's that simple. Which means you need to plan your pitches.

If you're pitching a news story to a blog or a newspaper and you have a specific release day in mind, start a week ahead from that day or date. If it's just an idea you have for a story—or you just think they'd like your client—do it before 4 p.m. If it's 4 p.m. EST, they're reaching the end of the day. If it's 4 p.m. PST, it's 7 p.m. EST. Basically, nobody's happy to hear from you.

How to Work with Others Who Want the Story

When you're really good at your job, people will come to you to find out more about your client. They want the scoop from you. Sometimes you can't give it to them. Maybe your client doesn't want you to talk about everything they're doing or planning. Maybe they do and you just don't know the answer to the reporter's question. In either case, it's always a good idea to use honesty as your policy. The moment you lie or withhold, you start to lose the confidence of those around you—your colleagues, your contacts, your network, etc. If you can't say what you're working on or you can't give a reporter what they're looking for (not yet at least), just promise that you'll get them everything when you have it. That's all you can (or should) do. The last thing you want to do is give out incomplete information that might confuse them. Your intention, of course, is not to confuse them, but when it happens often times it comes across as dishonesty. So be on the safe side.

For those reporters who always tell the right story and share how and what they say they will, it's important to reward them. Sure that's their job and they shouldn't have to be given a gold star and a ribbon for doing it, but that's not the world we live in. Though in fairness to the media, it's easier to do a bad job, so those who make the effort to do it right deserve some special attention. Give them the first glimpse at new products. Invite them to the client's place and show them around. Schedule a lunch with them and someone important on the client side. Give them behind-the-scenes details of upcoming events. Let them feel like you're not just some idiot PR person who has no interest in their success. Give them everything you can and more often than not they'll give you everything they can.

The more you monitor the media to see how various reporters treat your client, the better you'll know who to reward and who to avoid. There is no rule that says you have to pursue an equal number of reporters who are sympathetic and unsympathetic to your client. Those who are unsympathetic or not treating either of you well are not worth your time. You are better off finding other people with whom to share your ideas and your stories. Those are the people—the ones who produce the kind of coverage that is fair and, ideally, positive—who should get the best stuff.

How to Evaluate Success

At some point, your client is going to come knocking, wanting to know what you've done for them. When you first sat down with them, you talked about what they wanted from you and what they needed from your PR skillset. From there, you outlined a plan of attack: what needed to be done, when it needed to be done, and how you were going do it. That plan is the checklist that charts your progress. It shows that you are taking action and trying to follow a strategy. It also shows the client what has been done, what still needs to be done, and what might happen in the future.

As you begin to pitch stories born out of your mutually agreed upon plan of attack, create files for the positive, negative, and neutral responses to your efforts. You can take screenshots from social network feeds, you can collect email and phone responses, anything that does a good job of describing how the client has been received.

Show these files to the client with your notes. If things are going well, you'll look like a genius. If things could be better, include possible tweaks or strategic changes that should be considered and you'll look like you've had your finger on the pulse of the situation all along.

social media

When I was a kid, I was a compulsive liar. My life was pretty boring, average, and crap. I was all that you'd expect of the stereotypical nerd: 250 lb., heavily bullied, a shut-in with few friends who played an online wizards and goblins-type game called Everquest. I created stories that were just above the realm of normality—ones about meeting girls, going to parties, and other things that were plausible enough to believe but "cool" enough to make people think I was more than I was. Slapstick moments on my way to work. Meeting celebrities I didn't meet. Having more money than I did.

I was good at it, too. I was a good storyteller. I still am.

This trend continued into my first year of college in Aberystwyth, Wales, where I was bullied by housemates. I kept quiet. I made things up. It was easier than facing the truth. And I kept doing it until I studied abroad for a year at Penn State, a liberal bubble in the conservative cockpit of rural central Pennsylvania. I was able to start anew—I didn't have anyone there, I didn't have any reason to make up anything. And I learned that even my dumbest, stupidest moments could be told in a funny way—a truthful way—that was interesting. Suddenly, I became interesting, and it felt great.

Fast forward a few years, and I'm here in the PR hot seat. A company comes to me and says that their PR firm "exhausted the tech press," giving them no "ROI" (return on investment) and that in the end, the tech press was useless to them. I googled them. I used their app. I laughed, because they were so stupidly wrong that (to quote Louis CK) I nearly ripped off my ass, threw it at a wall, and jumped into another dimension. My client has an app that allows you to send whatever picture you've taken to the photo processing department of Walmart, CVS, Target, etc., with just two clicks on your phone. How cool is that? Can you believe that their old PR firm ended up with such a great client and produced such poor results? I can. It's because they couldn't tell the story properly.

PR—and social media to an extent—is all about being able to tell a story without being a lying, self-ingratiating dickhead. That means it's okay to post somewhat banal things on your social account (e.g., "making chicken parmesan" is fine, if not a bit bland) but posting ego-boosting, pretentious crap is a no-no (e.g., "making chicken parmesan with locally raised, free-range chicken, artisanal parmesan, fresh parsley").

Stay away from too many hashtags too. Using them because you read about them in a marketing book is a terrible idea. Social media is great and effective when someone is just themselves. I have about 3000 followers, and I post stupid crap all the time. But it's my crap. And it's funny crap. Yours doesn't have to be funny. You don't have to make up or embellish things to make them interesting, which I hope is what you have learned from this book so far, but the same goes for yourself.

You could be that fat guy playing Everquest. That's fine. Weight loss is hard. But don't go telling people you had sex with a hot MILF around the way when you didn't. Don't go on Twitter and start pretending that you're really into "media," or that you love X app or X show because your client told you to. Be you. Don't worry that you'll "make the client look bad" if you have an opinion on something.

Just reply to an ongoing conversation with something of worth. Get in there. Maybe they'll respond back, or retweet your stupid comment. Maybe they won't.

If you hear someone talk about personal brand, slap them. Personal branding is all a load of crap. You can't fake bits and pieces of you. Sure, if you want to seem good at something, post things of you being good at it. But don't wrap it all up into some personal brand story and try to appear important. My "personal brand" is that every time I have one of those off-thoughts that you usually don't say out loud, I put it on the Internet, for better or worse. The result has been mixed, but most people who follow me think I'm funny and retweet things I say.

Ultimately, social media is not going to make or break your strategy, because the client should be writing their own tweets. Teach them to be a normal human being and they'll do it well. Or, if they're a boring, reprehensible turd, that'll come out too. Nobody *needs* to be on social media. An electrician doesn't need to be on Twitter. An electricity company might need a Twitter account for answering questions, but they don't need one to "update people" on what happens to their company. Charmin (15,729 followers) doesn't need to be tweeting, and yet they have a stupid "verified" account tweeting variations on the idea that someone, somewhere took a shit and it has to be cleaned up.

The end goal with social media is that there is no end goal. You should not use it as if there is. Use it as a way to say things you're thinking about or to talk to people. Don't use it as a marketing loudspeaker. Nobody who matters cares. Someone retweeting about Doritos or your server architecture company or whatever sponsored tweet comes up in your feed is not going to give those companies a sales boost or make them better. That's just a fact, so embrace it.

The Downside of Social Media

Social media makes it easy to send messages out into the world, but it can also create problems in terms of connection. Too often we just blather on about whatever is at the front of our minds or what is most important to us. We don't think enough about what others want to see or what they'll actually respond to. When you're trying to connect with an audience on social media, you have to talk to them, not *at* them. It's an interactive dialogue between two or more sides. Unfortunately, we often don't interact. We just shout about ourselves and how awesome we are. This is where authentic engagement breaks down. And it's a recipe for being blocked, unfollowed, tuned out.

Think of social media as one big date. If you want to create a real connection with the other person, you need to show actual interest in what they have to say. They can tell when you don't and it usually means an early end to the night, with maybe a polite peck on the cheek and a brush-off at the front door. No amount of begging or boasting is going to get them to let you in and up to their bedroom, so maybe it's time to get to know them better, which means more time at the computer for you, PR pro. You can't engage without being part of the conversation.

The problems come when you have a large network of connections to manage. Your client could have as few as 300 followers or friends or fans, and even at one post per day that still means 300 new daily messages to engage. Who the heck can keep up with all of that? Even if your client is everyone's best friend in the world, and you read what everyone has to say, you can't respond to everything.

As a PR professional, your job is to put your client in a position to lead the conversation, find ways to capture readers' attention, and make them want to find out more. You want your client's audience to actually read the posts and engage in discussions. If not, you'll just get the scroll-by. And that means your hard work won't result in anything substantive. Which means you might soon be shopping for a cardboard box to live in, instead of a fancy apartment.

What you need to keep in mind is that people will make time for things they consider important in their lives. This is doubly true for things on the web, which is considered a leisure activity for most people. You need to grab people's attention, but on their terms, and on social media that translates into meaningful engagement and conversation.

Advertising Does Not Equal Communication

Advertising has saturated our lives like never before. Since many people have moved to watching TV online, traditional thirty- or sixty-second ad spots aren't playing as big a role in the lives of the audience. While this is a good thing for those who hate watching talking dogs in beer commercials, it doesn't mean they won't be annoyed by many other forms of advertising.

Remember banner ads online? How long did those last before people became irked by their existence? Two? Three seconds? The audience today is ultrasensitive to the placement of advertisements or anything that even sounds like marketing. But many marketers have decided to ignore this simple fact and continue to shout at their audiences, as though they're going to make an impression by being the loudest.

As a result, many people have begun to tune out anything from businesses, including social media campaigns. What can work to help reengage audiences is to think about how they connect with each other. They don't want to be sold to all the time; they want to be listened to and connected with. Do that as a business and the selling takes care of itself.

Beware of Users

As much as you might want to believe that everyone in your online audience is great and wonderful and has important things to say…it's not true. Most people suck. Many of them lead boring, pointless lives and use social media to write nasty things about your clients for their own entertainment. They can do things that create negative reactions within your audience, which can lead to PR nightmares. People use anonymity as an excuse to act like a dick. That's why people wrote death threats about me on forums when I reviewed the game Darkfall unfavorably and the company behind it claimed I played the game for only a few minutes. In fact, there's an Urban Dictionary piece about me. I have no idea who wrote it.

As a result, they often do more damage to the reputation of a company or a person than they realize. And because these actions might not impact their lives, it can be harder for them to feel any sort of responsibility. That is the problem with a tool that everyone can use: everyone uses it—for good and bad.

The Interaction Between Social Media and PR

Don't overestimate how well you know social media. Whether you embrace it wholeheartedly or have written it off completely is irrelevant. Just because you've posted a few things and your friends have posted a few things doesn't mean you really know what it does.

In fact, you might be guilty of some of the same faux pas that you will find in the following pages. This doesn't make you a shitty PR person. Social media is just trickier than it seems and often misunderstood.

What you need to keep in mind is that connecting is not the same as having an audience for a message. Having 10,000 friends online may make up for a less-than-stellar high school experience, but it will not mean you get a positive response to everything you do—and it certain doesn't mean those 10,000 connections are worth anything to your client. Sure, it looks good to have more friends than your peers, but if they're not sharing your messages and they're not staying engaged, they're worthless. They're worse than worthless actually, because they cost you money. It's like having a bunch of people you don't know come over for a party. They've come for the free food and drinks, but they're not chipping in for the pizza and you're left paying the bill.

Instead, the key is to find the right audience for your client. Find the right people and have a meaningful conversation with them instead of just bombarding them with marketing messages. Jared Newman at TIME/PCWorld has an Android phone. He loves Android. He wants Android stuff. Sure, he might mention the iPhone, but if you have something that does fantastical things to the Android interface, he's the guy to talk to. Not necessarily some guy who once wrote about an Android phone.

That is the audience you want to nurture. Social media users already hate that there are commercials and ads popping up in their feeds that they don't have any control over. Imagine how they will feel when a "friend" starts to yammer on about some client of theirs. It's probably not going to go well.

Think about how you can create authentic connections. Sure, that's total jargon-y buzzwords, but it's the truth. You're not going to become everyone's best friend, but you do need to engage with others enough so that they trust you. Give them help. Offer them something of value. Tell them a good story. Make their life better. Then, maybe, they'll trust you. And when they do, when they trust you, then you can talk about things that are important to your client.

The trust you build will be what sells the items your client hired you to promote, and it will be what people are acting on when they tell their friends about it. Accordingly, you shouldn't be trying to get people to buy what you're selling when you're on Facebook or Twitter or Instagram. Instead, you should be trying to entertain them enough that when you do have something to sell, they're ready with their wallets.

As a client, this is how you treat your customer. As a PR person, this is how you treat reporters or other members of your (professional) network. And make no mistake, social media users are a part of it too.

On Automation

As a busy PR person, automation is your friend. It helps you avoid some of the busy work that used to congest a large portion of the work day in years past. Your goal should be to use automation to be more efficient. It should not be used like a bot or a sock puppet, to do all the real work that you should be doing. *That* is a bad idea. Yes, there are ways to automate your posts. Yes, you can time things and set them up to keep going at all hours of the day and night. Yes, that is simple. And often free. But it is stupid.

First of all, does anyone think that you're online all the time? Nope. People realize when you're just automating things and letting the systems do the work for you. What often happens is that you set up all of these posts and you get lazy. You let things post at random times, thinking this will help get your client more coverage. And then you run out of your office, patting yourself on the back for being so darn efficient. And then someone responds to one of these automated posts, but you're not there to respond and communicate with them. Or worse, one of your unintentionally ill-worded autoposts goes out right after some major national tragedy and like that all your hard work goes down the drain.

The Boston bombing was yet another example of this. While people were desperately trying to tweet to find loved ones, see whether the country was being attacked, or just generally keep up with news, fast food companies and tech companies were tweeting inane updates. This (rightly) came off as crass and uncaring.

When the automation of your client's campaign leads to silence, your community will begin to fall apart. Why? Because you're asleep at the wheel. You're just letting posts occur at the "right" place at the "right" times, without any consideration for context or current trends. And when you're speaking for the client, your client is the one that's getting the bad reputation. Just putting a link out there isn't going to do your client any favors. Better to be a bit late with a response that comes from a real person than to be known for using bots to automate your social media presence.

Choosing Effective Social Media Platforms

There is no "one" way to approach social media, no matter what the gurus out there might have to say. Yes, there are certainly platforms where most people will be, but that doesn't mean you can or should be on all of them—or that any one platform will be the key to the success of your PR strategy.

Instead, you need to think about things like where your audience is, what they like to hear, and how they like to share things. Do they email back and forth, post links on Facebook, or share things on sites like Reddit or Digg? You will also want to think about how you enjoy using each of the social media platforms you sign up to use. If you're just signing up because you want to say you're on ten platforms, this is a bad approach. You're better off getting good at two or three and using them effectively. Here are the most well-known social media platforms you need to consider when putting together a PR strategy for a client:

Facebook

Is there anyone who isn't on Facebook? Even though it has become a little less exciting because of its overuse, it's still extremely relevant to your PR needs.

What you need to know about Facebook is that:

▶ It's common.

▶ It's more casual.

▶ It has opportunities for advertising and for businesses.

The most efficient use of Facebook for your clients is to set up a page for their PR campaigns. This might be a business page and it might even be run from a personal page, depending on who your client is and what they are trying to accomplish. With these pages, you will want to create unique and exciting profiles, ones that grab the attention of the reader and make them want to connect or "like" the page.

You can begin to highlight the power of the Facebook connection by talking about it in a blog or on the client's website. Yes, you might need to bribe or charm some people to get them to listen to you, but that's all a part of the game. Once you have developed some connections, ask them to share your page with others so you can connect with and tap into a larger community. This isn't going to happen overnight, no matter what you've heard. It takes time, patience, and diligence. Anyone who promises instant results is a scammer, plain and simple.

As you begin to share ideas and posts and status updates that resonate with your audience, you will begin to see more engagement and a network with accelerating growth. It can also help to reach out to the people who Facebook thinks you should connect with—hey, the buzz needs to start somewhere. You can also connect with other business pages and interest pages to start building a clear reputation for the client.

Facebook is not only a place to post your own thoughts (and your client's thoughts, of course), but also where you can share things from other people and use them to create conversations. Posting and sharing links, images, and videos is a great way to kick-start these discussions.

That said, you do need to make sure you're contributing to these discussions by "liking" things, sharing content, and answering questions or concerns. The more that you share and post on Facebook, the more your message will spread through different feeds, helping to bring in more interested people and networking possibilities.

Google+

Google+ is an acquired taste. Some say it's failing. Some say that Google has the resources to win out in the end. You want to seriously consider building something for it.

You can connect with Google+ users all over the world, and you can follow them all in a more defined way. What works well is to create a few "Circles" that are defined by the way they connect with your clients. For example, you might have a Networking Circle, which includes people who are interested in what you have to say. But then you might also have a Circle that includes people who want to know more about the company or client, so they'll be looking for more informative posts rather than just chit-chat. The trick with Google+ is that while the Circles allow for more security, they can also lead to a bit of confusion when it comes to how you share information.

You should have plenty of things to say about your client. Google+ is not the place just to post one thing and walk away. You need to keep posting and generating new conversations. You can respond in much the same way you do on Facebook, but you will also be able to use the +1 feature for your posts so they get more exposure outside your usual Circles.

You can have multiple Google+ accounts in order to generate buzz for different clients, so it's not something that you need to create a separate business page for like with Facebook. You can also link your Google+ page to Google Hangouts (an instant message system that allows groups to voice or video chat), Google Docs, and all of Google's free tools. It makes good business sense to have connections integrated with the world's dominant search engine. With the right SEO keywords and a groundswell of popular conversations, well-built Google+ profiles can and will boost your client's Google search results.

Pinterest

In terms of PR strategies for Pinterest, this might be the best tool for clients who have a focus on visual media. This isn't to say you can't use Pinterest for other clients, but there are limitations to Pinterest's technology and interface in terms of how your message gets out.

Pinterest allows you to "pin" images to different "boards" that can be broken down by theme. By creating different boards, you can define specific interest and market areas for your client that will further refine their brand. This attracts audience members who share an interest in what your client is doing and incentivizes them to share those specific boards, pins, and links with a broader and similarly interested audience. If they are a furniture company and their new coffee table is getting a lot of pins on people's interior design boards, this is not only a sign that your strategy is doing well but that your client has hit on something with this particular product line.

To create that buzz, just pin the right product images from your client's site and repin things you like (well, things that your client likes) on your own boards. You can also "like" other users' pins as well. This is the quickest way to build followers, especially on Pinterest, where a *quid pro quo* relationship can develop very quickly with Pinners looking to grow their audience as well. Don't misunderstand though; there's no way to game the system to get a lot in a very short time. This too takes time, patience, and diligence.

To use Pinterest, just sign up with the client's Facebook account, as this will integrate your posts with your client's Facebook profile. This keeps the conversation going, and it appeals to those audience members who are more visual creatures and don't just want to pour through words on a screen.

Twitter

Twitter has continued to play a significant role in fostering online conversation. You will want to begin with Twitter by following as many people who are related to the client as possible. This might be people who have the same interests, gurus in the industry, or just friends of the client. Again, you can start conversations with 140-character tweets, but then you need to follow those conversations to make sure they gain momentum.

Hashtags (denoted by the # sign) can be used to help define the things you want to share about your client. Be careful about overuse, however. Seriously, don't abuse them. Users can search for specific hashtags to help them refine the conversations they want to read, and spamming them with irrelevant hashtags is a great way to repel your potential audience.

Try to tweet useful things. Tweets should be funny, interesting, or newsworthy. Humor is always a big winner on Twitter, but make sure you stay within the boundaries of what's appropriate for the brand. Don't let your account post the same boilerplate marketing drivel. Yes, you are representing the client, but you need to tweet as if there is a real human being behind the account. Twitter will be one of the most human expressions of your client's brand and their social media presence, so you really need to get it right. Interact with followers, ask them questions, answer their questions, and respond to people in the industry. Make sure to retweet positive tweets directed at the client. This is a great way to make your followers feel heard, feel special. It's cheap validation but it works.

Do you follow everyone back? Well, yes and no. Your first instinct may be to follow everyone who comes to your Twitter doorstep, but when you do that you often end up with a quantity of followers that doesn't make sense for your client's needs.

If you really want to delve deep into who you're following/responding to, read the Twitter user profiles and the users' tweets. Take a look at who they are following as well to get an even sharper idea of who the account really is. In the end, it's not about the number of people you follow, but the number of people who follow you. They need to be active and engaged in what you have to say. You want people to "favorite" tweets that you post. This shows they're not only excited by what you have to say, but they also want to come back to that link or that message in the future.

The more that people retweet what you say, the more other people will see it, extending the message and increasing the possibility that you will gain more followers and/or notoriety. You can throw Twitter competitions as well. Give a prize to your one-thousandth follower for example—these can grow followers briefly, but you can't guarantee they'll stick around. Give them a reason to. Oh, and whatever you do, DO NOT BUY FOLLOWERS. Someone will find out, your client will get ridiculed, and you'll look like an ass.

YouTube

YouTube isn't for everyone, even though it seems like everyone and their mother has some kind of presence. Just because it's a great place to watch videos of kittens and people injuring their testicles doesn't mean it's right for your client.

YouTube works best for clients with the ability to show off their product on video. Tangible products in action, industry experts who can make engaging videos about their topic of expertise, and of course, those businesses that use viral videos to generate buzz (energy drink companies, extreme sports clothing brands, etc.).

When your client wants and needs to connect via video, the goal is to make sure as many people as possible see the video and share it with others. You can share YouTube links on Facebook and Twitter, as well as through other social sites like Reddit. You can also embed these videos on relevant websites, blogs, and any outlet willing to share the video. To begin using YouTube effectively, you need to set up a YouTube Channel. This will contain a description of your client and their business, and it can be customized with brand-specific color schemes and imagery to make it more compelling. People can subscribe to the channel to get notified of new videos, essentially making them instantaneous followers of your client's message.

YouTube works best when you post videos that are high quality. And while you might not have a degree in film, you can still make high-quality videos for your client with your smartphone or a small digital video camera. If you want to get serious about making a video go viral, this is something you need to keep in mind, and you may need to spend the requisite amount of time or money to see serious returns on a viral video. In the end you should prepare for the most likely result: your video won't go viral.

LinkedIn

Let's be realistic here—LinkedIn is a tool for presenting the most professional side of a client possible. And every client should have one, even the not-so-serious ones. LinkedIn is a place where an audience can find out exactly what a client does, what they have done in the past, and how they are impacting the industry.

Other ways to use LinkedIn include: Posting status updates (keep it to a more basic rundown of what the client is working on), getting involved in groups and discussions related to their industry, and of course, making network contacts.

Say what you will about LinkedIn, but a client's support of LinkedIn will lend them credibility online. It's professional, it's tame, and it's where networking happens. You can link it to your Facebook and Twitter accounts, so there is cross-posting potential as well.

Significantly, LinkedIn does not afford the same anonymity as Twitter and Facebook. It is a lot more civil and professional, due to the use of real identities and because its user base is not full of basement-dwelling young men or middle school kids. Use this rare bit of online tranquility to your advantage.

Blogs

While all of social media is going to be important in a PR strategy, blogging is still going to be important for a long time to come.

At the heart of it all, blogging is a platform for your client to talk about what's important to them. Unfortunately, there are hundreds of thousands of blogs out there so you have to make your client's blog really interesting, informative, and well-packaged to stand out from the rest. Make it worth something far beyond what your client finds interesting—think of what an audience or a customer would actually want to take the time to sit down and read.

The blog might include things like:

▶ Commentary about the news of the day.

▶ Longer posts about their thoughts or accomplishments.

▶ Details about events they led or participated in.

▶ Ideas about their audience.

▶ Personal stories.

117

When discussing a blog with your client, brainstorm five things that are most important to them in relation to their business. Then come up with a list of relevant blog topics that can support and encourage conversations over the long term related to those five things.

The way to be effective with blogging is to make sure your posts appear on a consistent basis, provide value to the reader in the form of well-written information or commentary, and make the reader feel as if their comments are being read and responded to.

Keep in mind that blogging works only when there is enough to say and there is an even greater commitment to keep talking. If the client is enthusiastic about the idea and you're not ready to sign on as a blogger, you might not want to start down this path just yet. The social media graveyard is littered with neglected, defunct blogs. Don't let your client's blog be one of them.

The Truth About Going Viral

"Going viral" isn't something that you can make happen. There is no special recipe for making something go viral, and there aren't any companies out there that can guarantee something will get popular. Well, alright, there are, but they come at an incredibly high price and you'd have to hire someone to do it for you.

You might know everything there is to know about the social networking world, but that still doesn't mean the video you created for your client is going to get popular.

Once you have posted something, sit back for a minute, grab your coffee, and see what happens next. You might hit the refresh button a few dozen times before you see anything.

You should always have a clear idea of which metrics you will use to measure the success of your social media campaigns. Is it page views, retweets, likes, shares, or comments? If you don't know beforehand, then you'll have no idea if the time and effort you spent was fruitful.

Don't beat people over the head with what you have to say. Start with one platform, then move the message to another and then another. You're trying to get something seen and considered, and that takes more time than you might realize.

You are also going to have to come up with new ways to share and spread the message. Your audience will get easily fatigued by seeing the same post, the same link, or the same tweet over and over again. But it's up to your wonderful creative facilities to figure out how to make that happen.

Control the Message

While you can post the message and you can make sure it gets out there, you also need to be ready to do any damage control necessary. When you're controlling a message, you're looking at how it has spread and how you can make it spread in other ways. For example, if you notice that a link has been shared on a certain site, you might want to engage in conversation on that site. You may even want to bring the conversation back to your client's site. But be careful. As I've said over and over again, audiences are very savvy and they can smell a rat instantly. If this backfires, all your work could go down the drain.

Controlling isn't about making people think a certain way, but it is about trying to ensure the right message is getting to the right places. This can help the message spread faster and farther than it already has.

If you're watching the movement of the links and the messages diligently, you will be the first to know when something isn't going the way you want it to. That's when your PR finesse will be needed.

And to be sure, you will have times when the information will get misunderstood, despite your best efforts. When this happens, you can step in, take the weight of the responsibility and move to clear things up.

Of course, speed is of the essence here, but what if you don't speak up as quickly as you should have? You can't be everywhere and some things just spread out of control, like a forest fire. But you now know what you can do to address these sorts of issues. Don't ignore them. Tackle them head on, do what you have trained for all these years (manage and repair your client's reputation), and everything will work out. People forgot about the whole "Tiger Blood" thing pretty quickly, didn't they?

building your own PR empire

It was CES, the Consumer Electronics Show, out in Las Vegas. One hundred thousand or so people were there to show off their prerelease wares in the hopes of getting press, booking orders, meeting someone. If you haven't been to Vegas, don't go. I like playing $5 blackjack, maybe a little craps, but that's it.

My former PR-self loved Vegas. I was wowed by the fact that everything was free. Going to a bar with people? Drinks are on the company. Meeting a reporter? Free drinks. Free meals. Free swag. Everyone's buying. Ostensibly I was there to schmooze with journalists, and the first night was always wonderful. I'd share a few beers, talk a little shop, and then go to bed at 10:30 pm. I wish I could say that's how the rest of the trip went down.

Instead, I'd wake up two mornings later feeling like I had been hit by a car that also flushed its exhaust into my lungs. This particular year, I vomited over the side of the bed (that my client had to pay for. Oops.). Half an hour earlier my chirpy, energetic manager called and asked me to come to the convention center as soon as

I could—no rush, but the sooner the better. I stumbled to my feet and, in what felt like the longest walk of my life, got downstairs (with a brief bathroom stop) to the cabstand. Every moment was pain. I looked back at the previous evening—clients, whiskey, blackjack—and one thought kept itself planted firmly in my mind: *This wasn't cool. I wasn't cool. This wasn't useful to the client or to my career in PR or anything, really.*

I eventually got to the convention center inside the Hilton, far away from the Las Vegas Strip. I felt nauseous and ran for the nearest bathroom, somehow vomiting again. The room was spinning and I realized that I was inside the former traveling Star Trek exhibition—removed from the Hilton in September 2008, ironically when I first came to America. With every swing of the door the room screamed "KAPLAK!" in my ears, taunting me in Klingon. I guess it roughly translated into "This isn't PR."

On that trip I met three reporters and hung out with the client a bit. That's about it. The client left our firm a few months later, not because of my drunken actions but rather because the results weren't there. The product they were showing off wasn't working too well, and reporters didn't like it. The CES trip was a failure, despite the bright lights, open expense accounts, and bottomless drinks. Then and there I realized that "location" is overrated. You don't have to be at every event, and you don't need to be a drunken, overly friendly asshole to make contacts or do your job. In fact, being at these giant shows is just a waste of your time, money, health, and youth.

Nowadays I sit in an office in Holmdel, NJ. I'm an hour from New York City. I don't think I've met with a reporter in over a year. I haven't been to a panel, conference, event, or major anything in forever, and my client base swells. I get new clients regularly. I make new contacts every day. I still have the same reach as big agencies but I get better results—and I don't just mean financial. While they're at the office until 9 p.m. and at every stupid conference and staffing booth, I am off work at 5:30 p.m. and I have lunch with my wife nearly every day.

What I'm saying is that we are within what I imagine the Global Village was meant to be, except I haven't read Marshall McLuhan and I probably never will. Nobody cares if you work twelve-hour days or 1.2-hour days. Nobody cares if you work from a gold-plated toilet on the moon listening to Lionel Richie on repeat. As long as you get results. If you get a client on TechCrunch when they want to be on TechCrunch and you get reporters to like you, all of which can be done via email and nothing else (using this book), you can do whatever you want wherever your want.

At my last agency, a friend of mine (who now works at one of the most successful/profitable games publishers in the world) and I made a fake PowerPoint slideshow called "Do Whatever PR." While partly a joke, one slide read as follows:

- "Strategic" is a stupid word that means nothing. We do whatever it takes to achieve results.
- We pitch the appropriate journalists with a legitimate angle about whatever it is you're selling.
- We tell you whenever your idea is terrible and will damage your brand.

> That's how I operate now. That's what got me to the position I'm in.

Company Man?

Some people are what the Boomer generation call "company men." They are loyal employees of an organization, willing to give years of service in exchange for a steady paycheck, the possibility of advancement, and, above all, stability. Does that sound like you? If the answer is a resounding "hell no" then pay close attention. This next chapter is for those who want to strike out on their own.

While you might not be one of those people who have "authority" issues, you might be the kind of person who just doesn't work well when they have someone hovering over them. You're creative and you want to make your own decisions. No matter how flexible some companies say they are when it comes to "collaboration" and "teamwork," most will have a leader in the end who slaps down dissent and makes the final decision. And you're often not a part of that decision.

Even if you're not fully able to support yourself with PR gigs just yet, you are at least on the path to independent success. Being your own guy or girl means the ability to manage your own time, say no (or yes!) to whatever clients come in, and take the full retainer for yourself. You will be the one who calls the shots and makes the big decisions—for better or for worse. This is a good thing, to be sure, but that doesn't mean it's easy.

What you do know is vast and great, but at some point, you're going to come across a situation you don't know how to solve. Your agency experience can only teach you so much. This is a different ballgame. You are a one-person show, and at some point, you will have to rely on others for their expertise, knowledge, or experience in dealing with situations you're not prepared for. What follows are the tools, tricks, and tips to building your own PR empire, one brick at a time.

Asking for Help as a Sign of Strength

Does that sound counter to the whole idea of working for yourself? You may have never heard this discussed before when people talk about entrepreneurship, but there's a reason for that. The idea of having a network of people to call on in times of need is so central to these lone-wolf types that it's not even worth talking about. To them, it's banal, obvious, and a part of everyday life.

Even Batman had a network he could call upon when he needed help. Your Alfred could be a virtual assistant who handles your calls. Your Commissioner Gordon might even be someone at a big agency, with big agency clients that can, at times, be useful to piggyback a pitch with (for example, a TV spot might fit your client that they've got you onto). Your Robin? That could be as simple as hiring someone in-person to do your basic document drudgery, all the way to finding a good partner to work with.

To do that, you're going to have to network. Networking will help you not only find people you can rely on, but also help find people willing to pay you for your expertise.

Business Development

Telling people "I have my own business" or "I run a PR firm" is great, but ultimately worthless if you don't have clients to pay the bills. And you're not going to get them if you aren't willing to put yourself out there to find them.

There are all kinds of ways to drum up business. Be thankful that I've tried them all and done the experimenting for you, so you don't have to suffer or fall behind on your rent.

I've done everything from cold-calling a company to blindly sending ideas to CEOs until they get back to me. I've publicly attacked companies that have become my clients. Of course, there's always the simple ones: someone said I was good at PR and sent a client my way. The cream of the crop will always be getting reporters to send clients your way—that's when you know you've made it.

Get Online

Getting yourself online is the most obvious place to start. Put up a simple website that lists what you will provide, why the client needs your services, and how you will work with them. It can be helpful to look at the websites of other PR companies to see how they're doing it. Then do the opposite. A lot of them use a ton of marketing jargon and bullshit that you should ignore. You want to separate yourself from them by coming across as honest, direct, and a pleasure to work with. Sad to say, but it's a unique position to stake out these days. A lot of potential clients will appreciate it, even if they don't hire you. They may end up telling someone else though, and that person might end up being your client.

Cold Call

Cold calling companies isn't as crazy as it sounds. If you notice a company being bad-mouthed online (and many are), reach out to them and offer your PR services. Talk about how you see their PR efforts failing and how you can help them out. Tell them exactly what you can do for them in the first 30 days. Note that when I say "cold call"

I don't literally mean "call them up out of the blue and pitch them on hiring you." Arrange a meeting with them, look professional, and come prepared. Again, they may not hire you, but they may be impressed enough to refer you to someone else who does take you on.

Start Small

Starting small is never a bad strategy. You can help out local companies who need PR for specific events or campaigns. This will help you build up a portfolio of work so you're not showing up for prospective client meetings without any experience. You can also find friends who are working on events, startups, or fundraisers and do some work for free. This gives you the chance to do some practical work in the field with very little risk to your own reputation.

Social Media

Get your social media profiles in order while you're at it. You need to be on Facebook (use a business page, please) and Twitter, at the very least. LinkedIn is also a very good way to make connections. You need to start posting your thoughts about PR and the ways you can help other people. Make sure your comments are insightful and interesting. And don't spam your friends and contacts with them either. If it's good, it will make the rounds and you'll get feedback. The more you show that you can effectively support your own marketing and PR efforts, the more others will trust you with their reputations.

Read

When you're not trying to drum up business, don't forget to keep reading. Learn everything about everything that interests you. Most

PR people are broken shells of humanity—people who have learned a few buzzwords and can make boring small talk. You want to be knowledgeable and a good person to talk to, whether at a networking event or a baseball game or a party. It's sad to say, but being noted for your intellect and personality is a serious competitive advantage in this field.

Your Portfolio

At some point, you will need to assemble a portfolio, both digital and hard copy, of what you've accomplished. What you need to do is to show that you understand how PR works and how you need to work in order to get noticed. Get together every single client hit you've ever made, any blogs you've written both for yourself and clients, and anything *you yourself* did.

Start a Facebook business page where you can grow your followers and show off what you have done and what you can do for other people. Share useful content, talk about what you've worked on, goals you've accomplished, events you've organized, social media campaigns you've executed, and so on.

Though it might feel like giving away insider secrets, you need to do it. There are plenty of websites idea poachers could browse (or stupid books they could read, heh heh) to learn what you have learned. If it's not your site they're looking at, it's one similar. You just have to get over that. If you have pesky little nondisclosure agreements, on the other hand, you may just want to talk in generalities about your client work so you don't violate the agreements.

It's important to realize that when you avoid talking about yourself and your skills in your portfolio, it is not humility, it's stupidity. Your portfolio is a reflection of your professional self. By excluding yourself from the conversation you are telling prospective clients that you have no clue what you're doing, that you might be incompetent, or worse, that you don't understand the basic concept of communication.

That last one is where problems really begin. The relationship you build with your clients is one that needs to be based on trust and rapport. The same goes for relationships with reporters, bloggers, and other influencers. You will need to get to know them well, as real human beings, and they have to trust you enough to know you're one of the good guys. Communication is at the foundation of all of those relationships.

Networking and Connecting

As we discussed earlier in the book, networking is one of the most powerful tools in your arsenal. You will meet all kinds of people who can help you and your clients in ways you cannot yet image. Your best clients, your most valuable information, and, in some cases, your most trusted friends and colleagues will all come from networking in one way or another.

What you need to know is how to do it properly. Too many people think it's about shaking hands and handing out business cards, or calling on people only when you need a favor. This is the worst way to go about it.

The notion that a good network is all about relationships may seem elementary, but that crucial concept is lost with most people. They think it's all about "what can they do for me?" and then "how can I get them to do it?" In fact, it's really the opposite.

Your best contacts will almost never be able to help you right away, at least not in any tangible sense. You'll meet them somewhere (often times in the most unexpected places), find you have something in common professionally, and then bond over something personal. Maybe it's a hobby, or a cultural background, or taste in food or art or music. When you meet somebody and think, "That's someone I want to keep in touch with" for reasons that have nothing to do with the business of PR, you can be sure they will be one of your most valued connections.

For example, Rip Empson at TechCrunch is someone who I have not run stories with in quite a while. Sure, when I first introduced myself in October of 2009, we ran a few here and there. However, for the most part, Rip is not my guy for most TechCrunch stories. Nothing against Rip—he's fantastic. But he also doesn't particularly like most of the clients I have. However, Rip and I keep in touch because Rip is a great guy who I have a lot in common with, someone I actually enjoy talking to, and someone who I value the opinion of. He's also sent me a bunch of clients. More importantly, he's been a good friend.

You must be open to discovering that relationship. It isn't something that happens upon you. It happens because of, and with, you. More importantly for our purposes in this section, however, make sure you nurture that relationship. Email them, call them up, take them out for coffee or a drink or dinner. Do not just "drop in to see how they are doing" when they are at work or at home. That's an invasion of their time and space and will make you look like a creep at best. Obviously don't pester them, but keep the relationship strong. Enjoy their company and absorb the indirect wisdom they'll pass along. Imagine that you're new in town and they're one of your first "native" friends.

One day, when you least expect it, they may call you up with a client they can't take on. They thought that you were the right person for the job and told someone to seek out your services. Or you may need to hire somebody to help you out when business is overwhelming you. Odds are they'll know someone who you can trust to get the work done.

This is why I am a proponent of networking the old-fashioned way—getting out there, meeting people, and keeping up some semblance of a personal life—rather than networking via a million anonymous social media contacts.

The Power of a Good Network

Even though I just described the wonders of networking from a warm and fuzzy point of view, let's take a step back and think about it from a more detached perspective. What does a good network help you achieve?

▶ More power.

▶ More influence.

▶ More opportunities to spread the word about you and your client.

▶ More opportunities to make connections.

In a broad sense, a good network is a tool for growing your PR prowess. The more people you know, the more you can do. On the other hand, a bad network won't promote your client, won't return your calls, and generally won't help you or your clients prosper. The key to a good network is the right connections. Without them your network is like a tree without a root system. It won't grow, it definitely won't spread, and it will eventually wither away to nothing.

That isn't to say that there are shitty people out there working to hold you back. Oftentimes, a bad network is far more benign. One example is your personal Facebook page. If you have a lot of "friends" who you don't know, then you'll often see little response to your posts. But if you have people who you really do know well on a real, human level, they will care about what you have to say and more importantly, they'll have your back when you need just that. If you have ten people in your network, but they give you good help time and time again, they're more valuable than the 300 "friends" on your Facebook page.

Having the right connections also matters when things don't go the way you intended professionally. A good network can create support for the client's next moves when the previous one was a misstep. They can step in and speak up for the client. They can make sure things don't get worse, sometimes even reversing the trend. A network can be a lifesaver.

When a client has had something written on a website that's incorrect, I've been able to reach out to reporters who don't work with me much but nevertheless knew me to get them fixed. Even if it's an article they didn't write, they were able to help me fix the situation.

The key is to NOT be a user of people. If you don't like them, don't force yourself to hang out with them. Don't laugh at their jokes if they're not funny. If you're not a fan, don't force it. Be friends with those you can be friends with. There will be the rare exception where you don't like somebody, but you will have to put up with them, lest you put yourself or your client in a situation with potentially negative consequences. You'll be able to tell when this is happening because it will feel like you don't have a choice. That's when you have to be a professional, suck it up, and make sure the client's check cleared. Otherwise, life is too short for shitty people.

How to Treat the People Who've Helped You

Everybody wants to feel like they make a difference in the lives of those they work with. Even more, everybody loves to be recognized for it. When you have a loyal audience or network that has seen you or your client through the peaks and valleys of life, you need to show your gratitude. That gratitude is like sunlight and rain, nourishing your growing PR empire.

Find ways to publically thank those who deserve it. From a client perspective, even something as simple as a post on a social network about how grateful the client is for having loyal supporters can go a long way. New audience members, new converts to your client's side, feel extra good about being recognized. And from there they often become even more vocal in their support for future endeavors.

A Note on Written Notes

I have a killer secret I use when I really want to go the extra mile for somebody. When I want them to know just how much I appreciate them, I...*wait for it*...handwrite them a note. It is a simple gesture that takes no additional time or effort and it absolutely blows people away. Nobody writes notes anymore. It's a relic of a more genteel era when people actually gave a shit about etiquette and manners.

If you want to be really slick about it, get some stationery or letterhead made. Most stationery shops will do thank-you notes with your name printed on some very nice paper stock. Letterhead is more for business correspondence but it can work. Write them something short and heartfelt. The only downside is you won't be able to see their reaction when they read it. And while most of your pitches and emails will get discarded, people tend to keep these sorts of things as mementos. Your goal is that they keep this gesture in their memory banks.

Rebuilding Bungled Connections

It's imperative that you treat everyone with as much respect and decency as possible. This is important for two reasons: 1) you're responsible for your client's reputation and 2) you're always trying to build and grow your network. Acting like an asshole or treating people with disrespect jeopardizes both of those.

Being a good person doesn't mean everything will go smoothly 100 percent of the time, of course. You will have encounters where things don't go how you wanted them to, or people don't react the way you expected. This can happen frequently with members of the media. You gave a reporter bad info or you gave someone else the scoop you promised them. Even though you need to be on your best behavior when you're in PR, you are still human and you will make mistakes. It happens.

If your client can't understand this—or you can't understand this—you're in the wrong business. Think about what might happen if your client makes a mistake. Do you immediately give up on them? No. You try to fix things.

I once had a client working in the home improvement industry. I had a trip to Florida booked for a few days and I neglected to tell him. When he kept trying to call me during said trip, I wasn't up front that I was actually gone; I was scared what he'd think. Eventually I came clean. The relationship was never the same and fell apart a few months later.

Just remember to be honest about whatever happened. Don't try to rationalize or justify. You won't learn from those mistakes, otherwise. Instead of wallowing in a pit of despair, soaked in vodka, think about what went wrong and how you might handle things differently in the future.

Did you say something snarky? Check in with whoever is upset with you. Find out from them what happened and what they think went wrong. You may find out that you didn't actually do anything wrong, and they were just having a bad day. The more information you can get, the more you can learn moving forward. If you did screw up, take responsibility for it. Let the upset party know that you realize you could have handled things better and that it won't happen again.

Make sure you offer a sincere apology. Even though you might think you'll save more face if you just move on, this is not what others want to hear. People LOVE apologies.

Send them flowers or a fruit basket if you really mucked things up. You'd be shocked at how few people try to make amends for their wrongdoings, let alone make any gestures expressing regret. A sincere, heartfelt phone call is also always appreciated.

Say what you will about mothers trying to get their kids to play nice with others, this is ultimately what your client needs from you. They need to know that you're building positive connections with everyone in the industry and that you will leverage those connections on their behalf. You do this by treating everyone well—even the ones you don't really like all that much.

Preparing for Future Success

Success is awesome. Getting more clients may mean more money, but it also means you need to give them an equal amount of support. This means more PR resources, which means you need to be ready to cry uncle when it gets to be too much. Right now, even before you have clients, you may want to think about the number of clients you can reasonably handle on your own. This will vary from person to person, but once you hit that number, it's time to consider hiring some reinforcements because you can't do it all.

If you think you can do it all, you're lying to yourself. You might be able to juggle everything for an extended period, but that almost certainly means you're not doing any one thing great and in total you're doing a half-ass job. At some point during your first or second year, you will notice that despite giving up sleeping, eating, showering, and your social life, you still can't keep up. Maybe you're missing deadlines, unable to manage your time or keep up with essential tasks like reading. However it manifests itself, when it happens you have to figure out the best way to bring in help. If you don't, I promise your client will catch on.

I'm really disorganized and prone to forgetting things. I had to hire an assistant firm—LongerDays.com—to handle my calendars, because I was legitimately forgetting weekly meetings on a weekly basis. I had angry clients. I had an angry wife who didn't understand why I was so on edge—and I was angry, because I was getting random angry emails and Google calendar didn't help. Now I've established a series of tools to accurately cover my own inability to keep time, both using a virtual assistant and to-do lists I read every hour on the hour.

If you have extra money, are free of debt, and can pay your personal bills each month, it's time to hire someone else. This person will help you have more time to bring in more clients, who will then pay even more, allowing you to make more. While it is a cost to pay someone else to do work for you, it's also going to help you be more effective for your clients.

If you're not quite there yet with your business, look into hiring contractors. There are tens of thousands of people across the globe looking for freelance work doing things like copywriting, editing, media monitoring, and social media. You can post job ads or go to freelance sites like Elance.com and oDesk.com, but the best way to find someone is to ask your contacts. That way, you're only dealing with candidates who've already been vetted on some level and you save loads of time.

Whichever way you choose to add needed help to your shop, the results are almost always a growing, profitable business. And giving people honest jobs is always a great thing to do, especially in today's economy.

It may be tempting to keep all of the pie to yourself, but there are two problems with that. The first is that at this stage, you really should be reinvesting everything you can back into the business. The second is that every business that really wants to go somewhere must expand. Apple wasn't going to be Jobs and Wozniak forever.

If you have no idea what your company should look like, take a gander at other PR company websites to see how many people they employ. Try to understand what the size of their staff means for their ability to handle client needs. Develop a staffing plan of your own based on your goals for your business, then think about how you can slowly expand to meet those goals. If you have a strong work ethic, it's not going to take as long as you think, which is why you need to be prepared for it.

This may not be the smoothest process, but it is essential to managing the growing needs of your growing client list. And that's what counts.

Management for People Who Have No Idea What It Means

Taking on people inevitably means having to manage them, with all the positives and negatives that come along with it. How ironic is it that you went out on your own to escape management, but now you're the one tasked with it.

But structure does have its benefits. You know this already. There's a reason millions of companies organize themselves in similar power structures: it serves some sort of purpose.

Structure brings accountability, something that every business needs. The thing to remember though is that the more rigid structures a lot of big companies employ aren't always right for PR. Relying on one person to approve every decision can be extremely limiting for the people on the bottom. It creates bottlenecks, frustration, even resentment. And if you ARE that manager, then you are the target of that frustration and resentment. From a personal perspective, what makes this most problematic is that you'll be busy answering questions as the face of the company, rather than doing the PR work you've been training to do. You came to PR and struck out on your own to be the person who helps clients, not the one who micromanages people's workday.

This sort of hierarchy also allows certain types to easily shrug off responsibility for decisions and tasks, especially when things go wrong. It's easy to send blame up or down the chain, and that can piss off a lot of people, especially when they're left holding the bag. And of course, PR being a creative enterprise, rigid structure does not sit well with the types of people who gravitate to the business.

Just looking at the ways you might want to promote a client's brand or message, you can see how being tied down to any one way of interacting or making decisions can be detrimental. Having to report to a boss every two seconds about what you're doing doesn't work in the world of social media, for example. It's not just annoying but totally impractical when certain actions must be immediate, and results are not linear and take a lot of time to surface. At the same time, PR is also a business that relies on carefully tailored, well-timed responses to problems and issues. You don't want to be justifying your existence to your boss when you really should be hitting the phones or monitoring some bad press about a client. In fact, this very situation is why many PR people do a lot of the work on their own.

Frameworks Are the Future

You need to have something different because you're doing something that requires specialized roles. Something that can move and flex with the things you do. You need a framework.

What the hell is a framework anyway? Well, if management is your parents, then frameworks are your cool aunts and uncles. They're still in charge of you and they still care about what you do, but they're not going to have the final say—like your parents did (and still do. Sigh.).

A framework is a structure of management that gives everyone a chance to speak up and be a part of the direction of the company as a whole. This allows everyone to be in charge of his or her own goals, but also collaborate on big decisions that need to be made.

No one person is in control, and no one person takes the blame when things don't go the way you intended. Yes, you can breathe a sigh of relief.

A framework might look like this:

▶ Different departments.

▶ Different working groups.

▶ Different focus points.

▶ Different time zones.

▶ Different client teams.

What can be helpful is for you to think about how you might set up groups of people in your company to manage these areas, based on their goals and skills.

This way, you can have the best minds together and the most focused minds in the same areas. They can interact with each other, support each other, and then reach out to other parts of the company when necessary.

For example, if you have a bunch of night owls working for you, assign them to your clients in Asia or Europe. They are going to do their best work at night or the early hours of the morning, so use that to your advantage. Don't make them drag their butts to work at 9 a.m. when they are sluggish and grumpy.

What you might want to do is to start one of those cloud-brainstorming charts, the ones where you write out all of the things that your company does and then you draw circles out from the main bubble to other bubbles that are related.

Your business is in the middle. From there, you might have different areas of interest for your client(s):

- ▶ Social media,

- ▶ Press releases,

- ▶ Newsletters,

- ▶ Presentations/public events, and

- ▶ TV and media.

When you look at the diagram, you'll immediately notice that some people are better suited to be in certain groups than others.

You may not be the best person for planning special events, for example. But someone on your team might be. Once you have the groups defined and filled up, you can more efficiently tap those resources on behalf of your clients. Not everyone will be involved at the same time, and that's okay. In fact, it's ideal.

After all, not all clients need the same things. Adding people for the sake of adding people just creates clutter. Even worse, if your client closely scrutinizes their bills, they might think you're trying to gouge them. The benefit of this kind of framework is that it creates quasi-think tanks that allow clients to best take advantage of your collective brainpower. No matter how you set things up, what you need to remember is that each person on your team needs to support your clients doing the things they do best. That is the key to a successful framework.

Certainly, a framework alone will not solve all of your problems. What it can do, however, is make sure you have the best possible team in place for the specific tasks you tackle on a day-to-day and client-to-client basis. You will still need rules and systems in place, but the more you can rely on a looser, more flexible group of leadership, the more likely you are to survive and thrive when the going gets tough.

Everyone Is in Charge

One of the best things about frameworks is that you have the opportunity to share power with everyone else. You're not the one who has to shoulder all of the responsibility, even if you take on the fancy title for the legal paperwork.

Create the sense that everyone is in charge and that everyone needs to act like their name is on the door. This doesn't mean they can boss each other around, but it should empower everyone with the ability to take charge of their projects and be accountable for their actions. The trade-off for this measure of authority is taking on a significant measure of responsibility for the success or failure of the company and any initiatives they've undertaken on behalf of clients. This is the price that your organization will pay for increased freedom. Your team cannot sit around and wait for someone to tell them what to do, not within this kind of atmosphere. They all have to take charge.

When you shift the attention to the overall goal, you really see the virtue of shared responsibility. You will want to drill into them the same credo I am trying to drill into you. It's the happiness of the client—not you—that matters. If this means one person who has a special relationship with the client takes over to smooth out a bumpy situation, so be it. Egos need to be put aside and that person needs to step up for the sake of the client and the morale of your organization. As long as you and your team remember that it's not about one person shining, but rather the entire company, then these moments should go off without a hitch.

There were moments when I worked with my science social network where things were slowing down. All of the pieces that I had that were running kept being pushed back and the people presenting the work (my work) weren't particularly sure how to present it. The client was ready to throw in the towel. Before I hadn't been particularly client-facing—I was the workhorse, after all. Instead, I was rolled out to discuss the actual, real situation in the trenches. My managers were nervous, but the conversation went fantastically well—the client appreciated understanding the process instead of hearing a bunch of marketing garbage.

Shared Blame

If you've set up a framework dependent on everyone working together, then your team should understand that everyone is going to share responsibility for what happens in the end, even if there was one person out in front. Obviously, no one wants to be wrong. No one wants to be the person who takes the blame for a mistake, even if it was a stupid mistake that deserves a little humiliation. At the same time, when you create an environment in which everyone has responsibility, they should already have bought into the notion that if the project gets screwed up, everyone was involved and so everyone needs to be a part of the solution.

Think about the last time you were in that office setting you left behind. When something went wrong, the person responsible was either humiliated or shamed in some way, or that person denied it forever and placed the blame on someone else. That kind of in-fighting and scapegoating doesn't really add up to a collaborative environment with the clients' best interests at heart.

When you have a framework environment, you foster the potential for creative collaboration and problem solving. No one person is to blame for anything that happens. And because of that, the problems you encounter aren't major issues anymore. They're just ways to come together to do something better. No one is cowering in the corner, no one is worried about losing their job because of a simple mistake. Instead, they bring it to the group intent on finding a solution. That's the idea, anyway.

Get Their Input

Creativity is what will keep your PR business alive. To facilitate that, it can help to put the coffee pot on and have brainstorming sessions among all of the groups. Even if the ideas that spring from these sessions are just silly, they are an opportunity to see how everyone works and to catalog ideas that might be usable in the future.

Write down all of the ideas, capture the brilliance of your teams. Keep it all in a document you can access anywhere, anytime.

Even if you already know how you're going to approach a client issue, asking for help may expose some angles you have not yet considered. Plus it invokes the spirit of teamwork and collaboration. If you just go through the motions and ask people for their opinions without actually listening or considering any of their ideas, people are going to catch on and tune out. Trust me, there are going to be some good ones that you want to use.

How to Make Everyone the Leader

The team that you hire needs to know they can lead too. At first, everyone is going to look to you for guidance. And you should provide it in terms of how you view the company, the direction you want to take it, how you want everyone to conduct themselves, etc. Beyond that, however, people should be leading their own groups or be asked to lead other groups. The more the leader role is rotated, the more people will get comfortable guiding others and being guided. It is also essential that people are able to run their own projects without input from others, unless they request it. They need to know that you trust they are making the best decision for themselves and the client. Make sure everyone has a chance at some point to lead something—even the people who want to be followers.

When you lead your company without acting like the typical officious manager and you put authority in everyone's hands, it's essential that you are clear about what you do and what you don't do.

For example:

▶ I don't make decisions about team projects.

▶ I do make decisions about budgets and business plans.

When you make clear what you are responsible for, you not only show the team how you're earning your money but you help them understand when they can ask you about different situations and when they should make the call themselves.

Even though the micromanager in you might cry when you see a team member going down a slightly wrong path, you do need to let them make mistakes. Obviously, you're not going to let someone do something REALLY stupid just to make a point, but you need to let people work out their own solutions to problems. It's the only way they'll understand *why* certain things worked and others didn't.

This wisdom gives them the confidence they need to keep working in their roles, knowing they can tackle anything. After a mistake is corrected, you might want to sit down with the people responsible to see what happened and what they might have learned from the situation. You can even problem solve to see how something might be handled a bit better in the future. That will be the true value of your leadership at the head of the company.

The Power of Personal Authority

Authority is the idea that you have your own innate power. When you have this power, you are able to make your own decisions and are expected to do so based on what you know and what you think. This does not necessarily involve having power over other people; it's more about having the power to do what needs to be done. When it's understood that you have power, you need to be ready to use it well.

The basics for using power well are:

▶ Don't use power to manipulate.

▶ Don't use power to control.

▶ Don't use power to harm.

Your PR team needs to know they are not only responsible for what they do, but they are also responsible for the impact it has on others. This is a critically important point because power can go wrong. It happens all the time in every arena.

145

Sometimes, we just want to do things the way we want to, and that's that. To get it done, we can choose to be a jerky boss or we can choose to persuade. While it might seem expedient to use brute force or power plays to get the immediately desired result, this typically leads to hurt feelings and alienation; the sense that those in power are trying to coerce those beneath them. Often, this is the result of something bigger than ego. It stems from people who don't know how to wield power properly, or those who have been manipulated in the past. Not only is this wrong, but the people who feel manipulated now are not going to be available in the future when you need them most.

Try working *with* others on a mutually agreed upon goal instead of trying to *make* them work for you. That's when you typically see the best results and you create a friendly work environment in the process. If you can go back to the idea of the framework instead of a structure, you can see how the collaborative model can be helpful. Working together allows everyone to have power and a chance to be in charge at some point.

Fortunately, if the framework exercise is successful, your team won't rush to power. They will already feel like they have authority and are making a contribution to the organization and won't feel the hunger to be in charge just for the sake of it.

In the beginning of your PR business ventures, it might be reasonable and necessary for you to be the one in charge. When that happens, you need to act with respect and empathy. It's the only way to create a model for others in the organization to follow who want to step up to the plate. Handing over leadership at opportune times is a good move. It shows that you're secure enough to let someone else make decisions and it allows you to focus on other things. Try it sometime.

Learning How to Use Your Authority

Before you hand off authority to other members of your team, it's important that you know how to identify and handle situations where you need to step up and take control. You should step in as a strong leader when things are hard. It's your company and your team, after all. A great way to check yourself is to see if these steps can be followed first:

▶ Can the person work it out on their own?

▶ Is the client unhappy?

▶ Is there anyone else to handle the problem?

▶ Did somebody do something wrong?

The reason you want to ask these questions is to ensure the other team members have a chance to work things out on their own. They need the chance to work things out without your intervention.

When a situation arises that requires your leadership, make sure you are consistent with your decision. Follow through on what you say you are going to do and then discuss it with your team afterwards. Deal with things as soon as possible and give yourself time to talk things out after the emergency has ended. If this happens more than a few times, it might be necessary to get a new team, but fortunately the feedback process will help train others how to not screw up. That's the benefit of empowering your staff to think and act for themselves

Learning from Your Management Mistakes

Many people think that being in charge means that you put your feelings aside and focus on the work. I wish I could say that were the case, but it simply isn't. You want to take things personally as a leader. You want to make sure that everything you do is important. Every decision you make counts. It should matter to you personally. You should be upset when things don't work out. Does this mean that you should cry in a corner for the rest of the day? Of course not.

You can take things personally and not let them hold you back. You just have to learn from them. This will prepare you for the next time something like this comes up.

When You Do Something Wrong

In my past jobs I've seen management fail to understand when we've lost a potential client after a seemingly successful meeting. We failed to land a huge file-sharing software client because they went with a more "tech-specialized" agency. We did exactly the same thing. The problem was one of perception.

What management saw was an inspired room of their workers talking vividly about the potential client with angles that would be a great success, with a stubborn CEO who would not see things our way.

What I and the client (I knew them, and they told me in confidence) saw was a room of PR people who vaguely discussed ideas that barely approached actionable tasks. When members of our staff were challenged on knowledge of the tech industry, they were vague, constantly said "um" and "like," and didn't gesticulate with any level of deep knowledge.

Furthermore, when clients left our agency to go work with another, it was blamed on their own personal relationship with the client or lies that they'd told. The truth was that our results weren't stunning—and our personnel weren't charming or incredibly knowledgeable. We weren't not getting these clients against the big agencies because we were seen as too small—we were babbling endlessly in meetings to the point of boredom.

You at times will have to look deeply at your work and yourself and judge objectively whether you performed well. If you didn't, you absolutely have to learn. And do better. Even if a client leaves, being a good loser will benefit you in the future. Hell, they might even come back.

When a Client Does Something Wrong

When a client does something wrong, many PR agencies fail to even say that they're annoyed. They marketing-speak their way out of the situation and don't seem that annoyed. What really needs to happen is a frank discussion of what's going on, and you need to level with them about why you're upset.

During these situations, it can be a good idea to talk to the client about how upset you are. While you don't want to cry on their shoulder, you do want to talk about how important it is for them to succeed. This will show that you are taking things personally.

Then, you can take them too personally. For example, a client of mine that helped organize your email inbox out of nowhere had someone I didn't know pitching them. By pitching, I mean they sent out the same, horribly written email to 300 reporters, some of which I'd already pitched.

I admit I overreacted and sent them an email that simply said, "what the fuck?" and had the text at the bottom. I threatened to fire them. This was not the right way to go.

Another example was when I had a financial services client for whom I got a piece on USAToday.com. The problem? I was quoted in the article as their spokesperson. This didn't go well with my boss or with their boss. I desperately asked the reporter to remove it—he didn't.

In the end, the client was flipping out, and I simply called them and said the truth: That ultimately this wasn't a huge deal, because even if I was a quoted spokesperson over one of the clients' staff, it didn't make the message any less powerful. When the client was shouting, I nearly cracked and said something I might regret. Instead I stood my ground, said I'd done nothing wrong (they said I had made myself the spokesperson), and they cooled off.

While they were slightly uptight, the client eventually understood.

Some lesser PR people might let one bad rating or write-up ruin their whole strategy. You don't have to be that way. But when you stop taking things personally, then you might need to take a break. You are standing up for your client's needs. It is personal, so react accordingly. And it certainly is professional to recognize when you need to get your head back in the game.

Overstepping Your Boundaries as a Boss

Before you get overly optimistic about frameworks and leadership, let's look at what's probably going to happen first. You're going to get so wound up about being in charge or about the possibility of being in charge that you're going to overstep your boundaries and act like a dictator.

And you're going to feel completely justified. Whether you believe it or not, it happens, and it will happen to you too.

When it does, you need to take actions to repair your newfound reputation as a douchebag. Luckily it's not hard. Apologize sincerely, ask for feedback, and don't do it again. It's no different from when you messed up with a client back in your agency days (that did happen, right?).

Take responsibility for what happened and how it happened. Be clear about the fact that you know you screwed up. Then, if you need to, apologize personally to those who you might have run over during your power trip. Be clear with each of them that you regret your actions and that you want to get past this moment of ill thinking.

And while you might want to just leave things at this, you also need to listen to the feedback team members might have for you. Listen to it and understand how they perceived the incident. And most importantly, don't do it again.

Can You Give Your Team Too Much Freedom?

Your leadership instincts might make you wonder if letting your team do whatever they want is a good thing. You want to believe that they are making the best decisions, and you want to show that you trust them. But something is nagging you deep in your gut. As Ronald Reagan said, "Trust, but verify."

Here's where you need to get a little sneaky. You still need to have accountability among your team members. Whatever the metric may be, you need to know that your team is doing what they're supposed to be doing.

When your team members are working on projects for clients, let them know that you will need updates at regular intervals. After you make this request, start asking about the project every few days. This will ensure the team is always ready with a status update for you and the client. The key here is to check in less frequently over time. This will keep your team on their toes, without driving them up the wall.

You can also check in with the client and see how they're feeling about the project. Not only can you do this, but your team should be doing this as a part of their job as well. You may want to ask new team members to write up short summaries of the things they did in an email each day. Yes, it's busy work and they'll whine about it. Yes, you will whine because you have to read all of these reports. But this action will create some accountability for the people in your team. Even if they didn't do much, you will have this recorded for future consideration.

Some organizations ask team members to fill out timesheets that itemize the specific tasks they accomplished during a typical day. Lawyers in particular are known for this. Most bill in six-minute increments. It may seem a little OCD, but it's one possible tool you can use if you feel like the team is slipping.

Try to have an instant messaging system up when all of you are on the clock. Even though you might not need to talk to each other all day, you can at least have the opportunity for it to happen. You can poke at someone who you think may not be working as hard or as much they should, and see what they are up to.

It can also be helpful to have face-to-face feedback sessions at least once a month to see how things are going. This will help you have a better understanding of what they need from you and what they might want to learn from you. In this sort of conversation, it's not just about what you want them to know, but also about what they might need to be trained in. As a result, it becomes a development session in which you get a better team member with the skills to do their job even more effectively.

Your team aren't the only ones who need to be empowered. You might want to have a little chat with your client too. Let them know that while you are the PR professional, they are a vital part of the ongoing conversation. Let them know that they are just as much a part of this process as you are and that their feedback is welcome—no matter how blunt or unpleasant. You want to be embedded in what they're doing to the point that it personally matters—it'll make you better.

in conclusion

PR is oftentimes made into a monstrous entity bereft of personality and humanity. People are afraid to show their true colors, their true opinions, and who they are as a person. The truth is a strong foundation either as a manager and a subordinate or a PR person and a client can be built on having a truly personal relationship.

When I was at my last agency, I managed a colleague of mine called David. He loved games. He didn't know how to pitch. We'd enjoy talking to each other a great deal and had a great rapport that meant when I had criticism for him it wasn't taken as a harsh chiding. He'd listen to me because he knew I cared—not because I was his report, or because I was "better" than him. He wanted to get results like I did, and he listened to what I had to say. He's still working at the agency and is a fantastic PR guy.

When I call Joe Ariel of Goldbely (a curated marketplace for amazing food), we often speak for over an hour. Usually it's thirty percent actual client deliverables, and the rest about amazing foods we've tried in the past, or things he's bringing to the site. We might veer into the world of our personal lives. We might talk about things we've read. What we do the entire time is have an honest and enjoyable dialogue about what we're working on. I'll talk about when things are tough. He'll talk about what he wants from the next month. It's not a formalized or rigorously structured meeting—but we get a lot done because we actually enjoy the conversation.

It's incredibly scary to open yourself up to somebody even on a very superficial level. They might know things about you that you want to hide—you might be disorganized, or overly emotional, or you might not have great news for them about an article that's no longer running. The truth is that surrendering yourself to the process and having these open, honest relationships will pay dividends in trust between you and another person. That could be professional. That could be personal. Regardless, it will help you rise above a cloud of people who do not open themselves up to their clients or their workmates. Workmates may find it weird—even off-putting—but I've never found a client that didn't appreciate a personal and honest working relationship.

epilogue

When I wrote this book, I set out to provide PR newbies with as much information as possible to help make their entry to PR a little less stressful. What you have read is a collection of my battle-proven thoughts, strategies, and information—not to mention a rundown of my screw-ups, illustrated in all their glory precisely so you can avoid them.

I love my work. There is simply no other industry I'd rather be in. Even though I am at the point in my career where I have my own shop, I still love to meet new people, talk to my team, and of course, pitch.

Many people get discouraged or burnt out and decide it isn't for them. There's absolutely no shame in that. Those people should be commended for having the guts to admit it wasn't for them and move on to something else. Most people would be too scared of being considered a failure, of being judged by their friends, family, and colleagues, to ever contemplate that.

My hope is that if you do decide to stick it out in this great industry, you will carry forward with the same enthusiasm you have now, and I still hold in my heart. We all have our bad days, and you will have some very bad ones in the not-so-distant future—I know from experience—but with your own resilience and determination, not to mention the advice I dole out here, hopefully you'll weather the storm. Or better yet, avoid the storm in the first place.

~ Ed

Made in the USA
San Bernardino, CA
05 January 2018